Klee

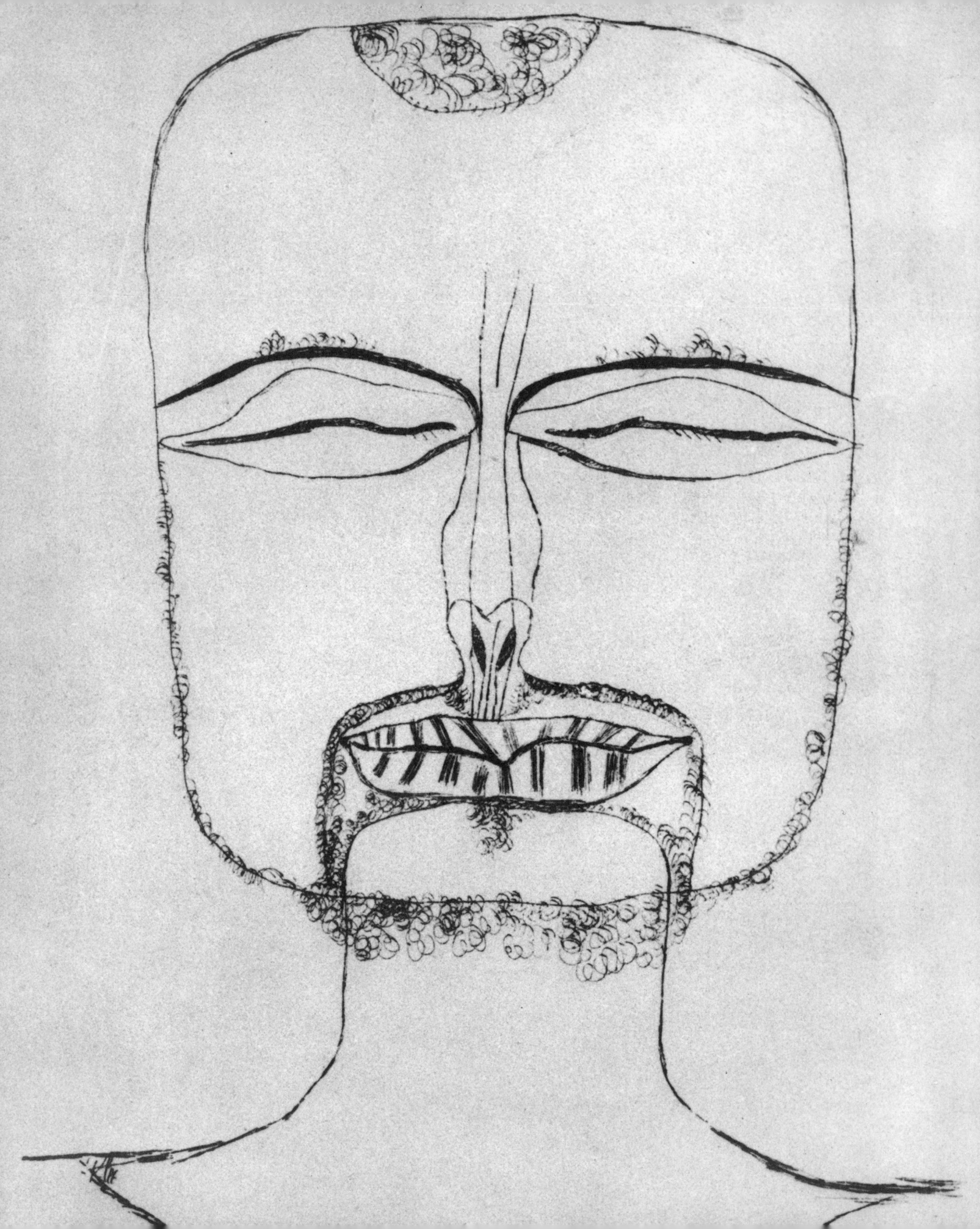

SPRING ART BOOKS

by Norbert Lynton

SPRING BOOKS · LONDON

ACKNOWLEDGMENTS

The paintings and graphic works in this volume are reproduced by kind permission of the following collections and galleries to which they belong: Kunstmuseum, Basle (page 17; Plates 15, 18, 23, 26, 32, 45, 50); Kupferstichkabinett, Basle (Plates 8, 43); Albright-Knox Art Gallery, Buffalo, N.Y. (Plate 35); Ralph Colin Coll., New York (Plate 13); R. Doetsch-Benziger Bequest, Basle (Plates 8, 18, 23, 43, 50); Mrs T. Durst-Haass Coll., Muttenz bei Basel (Plate 19); Kunsthalle, Hamburg (Plate 24); Emanuel Hoffmann Foundation, Basle (Plate 32); Lady Hulton, London (page 35; Plates 4, 11); Felix Klee Coll., Berne (Plates 2, 3, 5, 9, 25, 27, 39, 40, 46, 47); Klee Foundation, Berne (Frontispiece, pages 8, 17, 18, 21, 24, 25, 36; Plates 1, 6, 10, 12, 16, 20, 28, 29, 30, 31, 33, 34, 36, 37, 41, 42, 48, 49); Ida Meyer-Chagall Coll., Basle (Plate 45); Museum of Modern Art, New York (Plate 14); Philadelphia Museum of Art, The Louise and Walter Arensberg Collection (Plate 22); Phillips Coll., Washington (Plate 38); Galerie Rosengart, Lucerne (Plate 44); Peter A. Rübel Coll., Cos Cob, Conn. (Plate 7); Herman Rupf Coll., Berne (Plate 21); Mrs Jane Wade Lombard, New York (page 25); Yale University Art Gallery (Plate 17). The painting reproduced on Plate 19 was photographed by Photographie Giraudon, Paris; Plates 8, 15, 18, 23, 26, 32, 43, 45, 50 by Colorphoto Hans Hinz, Basle; Plates 4, 11 by Michael Holford, London. Plate 3 by Werner and Suzanne Killian, Vienna; Plate 24 by Ralph Kleinhempel, Hamburg; Plates 2, 5, 9, 28, 29, 39, 40, 46, 47 by Jacob Lauri, Zürich; Plate 25 by the Museum des 20. Jahrhunderts, Vienna; Plate 27 by St. Thomas University, Texas.
All plates are © S.P.A.D.E.M., Paris, 1964

The design on the back of the bookjacket is reproduced from Paul Klee's drawing Woe, woe (*Ach aber ach*) 1937 by kind permission of Rolf Bürgi, Berne

First Published 1964

2nd Impression 1966

Published by
SPRING BOOKS

Drury House • Russell Street • London WC2
© Paul Hamlyn Ltd 1964
Printed in Czechoslovakia by Polygrafia, Prague
T 1680

Contents

Black and White illustrations (see notes on pages 38-9)

The source of each quotation has been indicated. For the most frequently drawn-from sources I have used abbreviated forms of reference, as follows:

J: Klee's journal published as *Tagebücher von Paul Klee 1898—1918*, edited by Felix Klee, Verlag M. DuMont Schauberg, Cologne 1956 and (paper-back) 1957; plus section number and (unless already stated) year.

FK: Felix Klee, *Paul Klee*, Diogenes Verlag, Zürich 1960; plus page reference.

MK: Petra Petitpierre's stenographic selective record of Klee's teaching in Düsseldorf, published as *Aus der Malklasse von Paul Klee*, Benteli-Verlag, Berne 1957; plus page reference.

EPK: Reminiscences of Klee written by friends, students and acquaintances, edited by Ludwig Grote and published as *Erinnerungen an Paul Klee*, Prestel Verlag, Munich 1959; plus page reference.

ESB: Lothar Schreyer, *Erinnerungen an Sturm und Bauhaus*, Verlag Langen-Müller, Munich 1956; plus page reference.

I should like to record my gratitude to Mr Felix Klee and to the Director and staff of the Klee Foundation in Berne for their help.

Introduction

Klee's statement that 'there is far too much concern with biography in art' has sometimes been quoted; less familiar is his opinion that 'an artist's way of life, as seen from the outside, can tell us much about the character of his creativity' (J 861; 1909, and 958; 1915).

Rather than present a detailed biographical account of Klee's life, or attempt in metaphysical or pseudo-philosophical terms to elucidate the meaning of his art, I have thought it best to concentrate in my introduction on his development, merely outlining the biographical framework within which it took place, and leaving almost all comment on specific works to the notes on the plates. This development is principally the story of his long struggle to become a painter. Once he had reached the point at which he could consider himself a painter (about the age of thirty-five) he did not so much go on developing as extending his range, so that I have concerned myself in much greater detail than other writers with the years up to and including the first world war. From then on it is principally the paintings that count and I hope that the plates (and the notes) will complement the emphasis of the introduction. I have also included short sections on some selected aspects of Klee's work, ideas and personality, under separate headings.

In all this I have drawn very heavily on Klee's own writings and on the published reports of Klee's friends and acquaintances—especially on the journal which Klee wrote till 1918 and which, although available in print since 1956 to anyone who can read German, seems to me to have been used only very superficially. The reader will find a great number of quotations (and a few poems) that have never before been translated into English; if the English in which he reads them seems to him sometimes stilted and inelegant, this is because I have tried to stay as close as comprehensibility will permit to the original, which in Klee's case means a German rich in idiomatic usages and idiosyncratic word-play. Klee was a highly literate man who could, I believe, have made a career for himself as a writer.

Paul Klee was born at Münchenbuchsee near Berne in Switzerland, on December 18, 1879. His father was a German, a music teacher. Paul grew up in Berne and attended the municipal grammar school until 1898. Probably the most significant aspect of his childhood, apart from the musical atmosphere of his home, was the richness of his imagination: fairy-tales, daytime and nocturnal fantasies—these things occupied his mind more vividly than they seem to do in the averagely imaginative child. At any rate, he was able to write about them later, remembering even the dreams of early childhood, such as the evil spirits which he drew at the age of three or four and which then came to haunt him (J 10). At school his favourite subjects were botany, mathematics and ancient languages (FK 44). He assimilated knowledge and skills with considerable ease, so that when he left school and had to specialise for the sake of his career, many fields were open to him. Although he was by now a proficient violinist, and assisted as such at orchestral concerts in Berne, he hesitated to make music his career partly because he recognised in his violin teacher a sad and frustrated soloist. He wrote poems and short stories but came to see his leanings to literature as the expression of a profound poetic instinct that could not interfere with, and could well support, creative work in the plastic arts. About these, he wrote later, 'there was something tempting, even if at first it was not art as such but rather the expectation of being able to get far away, out of Switzerland, to somewhere where life was bigger, more interesting and more alive.' He had to choose between Paris and Germany; Switzerland had no significant artistic centre or tradition. Germany appeared to him more congenial, and so in 1898 he went to Munich, into the private art school of Knirr as preparation for the academy.

At Knirr's he enjoyed himself, doing a good deal of life drawing and inventing compositions on epigrammatic themes. He was soon considered one of the most promising students, but he himself seems to have been concerned with personal problems rather than painting: 'I hardly think of art; I want only to work on my personality' (J 83; 1899). But almost without his being aware of it art established itself as his way of life while he

Drawing with the fermata

found his feet in the world of human relationships. In the autumn of 1899 he met the pianist Lily Stumpf. She, three years older than Klee, did not at first encourage his devotion, but it seems to have helped him find his way through the maze of late adolescence. In 1906 they were married and in the same year Klee had his first exhibition. In 1900 he had transferred from Knirr's school to the academy class of Franz Stuck, one of the most admired painters and the most reputable teachers of Munich at that time.

To be Stuck's pupil sounded very splendid, but in reality was not half so wonderful... In the field of colour I made scarcely any progress. Since my handling of form was strongly dominated by emotion I thought at least to be able to profit in this respect. There was really much to be learned from Stuck about that. Of course it was not only I who lacked something as regards colour: Kandinsky, a fellow student, but Klee knew him only slightly at this time, said much the same in writing about this school later. If Stuck had analysed the essence of painting for me in the way I was able to do it later, after I had gradually searched my way into it, then I would not have found myself in so desperate a situation. I wondered what might otherwise be achieved through this influential man. I brought him illustrations for his opinion and he thought them exceptional. He suggested I should try offering them to *Jugend*. *Jugend* at that time did not want to know about me (J 122; 1900).

Munich around 1900 was the leading centre in Central Europe for the modern style in art and design, *Art Nouveau*, known in Germany as *Jugendstil* after the magazine which propagated it. Unlike Kandinsky and others among his contemporaries, Klee does not seem to have been particularly influenced by it although he must have felt the breath of fresh air which the movement blew into German art and have been helped by the emphasis it placed on the expressive potency of form and colour as such. Stuck meanwhile encouraged Klee to turn to sculpture—'Proof that he really knew nothing about colour' (J 140;1901)—and Klee applied to the academician Rümann for admission to his sculpture classes. As a student of Stuck's he expected to be admitted without ado, but Rümann, who seems to have been a rather difficult old man, insisted on a special examination which Klee refused to take, and so the idea was dropped.

In 1901 Klee went to Italy and spent there about twenty-seven weeks, from October until the beginning of May 1902. He visited Milan, Genoa, Pisa, Rome, Naples, Pompeii, Florence and several other places, studying, working and looking around. The journal is full of revealing comments. In Rome 'Michelangelo had the effect of a whipping on the pupil of Knirr and Stuck' (J 285;1901). The naïve style of certain Early Christian works in the Lateran Museum moved him, on the other hand, much more than the perfection of Michelangelo's *Pietà*. He envied the ancients their knowledge of the nude and bought a set of photographs of Greek and Roman sculpture in the Vatican. Perhaps stimulated by these he joined a German art group in January and attended frequent life classes; at the same time he decided that next winter, in Berne, he would study anatomy thoroughly 'like a medico' (J 341;1901). He did in fact attend anatomy classes in Berne in the winter of 1902–3, starting on November 1 and going every morning from half-past eight until-half past ten. From March 23, 1902, until April 6 Klee was in Naples, from where he made a three-day trip to Pompeii, Positano and Amalfi. He was fascinated by what he saw in Naples Aquarium, the 'snake-like monsters with poisonous eyes, enormous jaws and maws like pockets'. Some 'squatted with the sand up over their ears, like prejudiced humans. The common polyps look like art dealers; one particularly eyed me in a familiar, compromising way, as though I was a new Böcklin...' (J 390;1902). The Pompeii frescoes, with their emphasis on silhouette and their elegant, decorative colours, seemed to him to come especially close to his own artistic personality. 'They were painted for me, excavated for me. I feel myself strengthened' (J 391;1902). He then had a few more days in Rome, visiting Tivoli, seeing the annual modern art exhibition where he was excited by what he called Rodin's 'life caricatures', and having a final look at Roman antiquities. On April 16 he was in Florence. He was overwhelmed by the Uffizi Gallery, both in quantity and quality. He found Botticelli to be a greater colourist than he had been led to expect. He saw Egyptian and Etruscan antiquities in the Archaeological Museum, as well as a section of Gobelin tapestries. He visited the Bargello and the Museo dell' Opera del Duomo, where he was impressed by the Renaissance sculptures, especially those of Donatello. Michelangelo's Medici Chapel earned his highest respect but also repulsed him on account of its aesthetic coldness. On May 2 he left for Berne: 'at home I found everything in order, a good bed, meals provided without tips, two charming cats, Miezchen and Nuggi, grey on grey' (J 409; 1902).

What did Italy give the young, searching artist? The first thing to notice is that he gave Italy priority over Paris, just as he had given Munich priority over Paris earlier. To an extent that may surprise those who know Klee only from his later work, he had in him a leaning towards classicism and the humanities that drew him to Italy and which Italy confirmed. He studied classical sculpture. He read classical authors in the original languages. From Renaissance architecture he learned 'the architectonic (today I would say the constructive) aspect of art' (J 429; 1902). The architects' concern with the proportional interrelationship of the parts of their buildings helped him to understand 'the numerical element in the concept of an organism'; this facilitated the subsequent study of nature which, much more complex, is nevertheless comprehensible in the same way (J 536; 1903).

Altogether Klee returned much strengthened. He was soon to find, however, that his classical leanings made it difficult for him to achieve artistic independence in that it inhibited him from moving beyond naturalism. The unmistakable originality shown in his first extant graphic works was reached gradually and with great effort: Klee had to surmount his own skill as life and landscape artist.

Until 1914 he worked principally in the graphic media, and in so far as he gained any kind of reputation before the first world war this came from exhibiting and occasionally publishing drawings and etchings. It is clear, though, that it was his intention to be a painter and that throughout his first decade as a practising artist he kept on experimenting with oil paint, sometimes with oil paint in combination with watercolour, although scarcely anything of this kind remains. In June 1903 he described himself as 'at present a very weary painter but otherwise a continually potent graphic artist' (J 512). He understood instinctively that colour was for him the problematic element in painting. There is plenty of evidence that he was particularly sensitive to colour but in spite of this (or because of this) and in spite of his searching colour studies from nature, he could not for some time handle colour to his own satisfaction.

The satirical etchings which are the chief remaining products of the years 1902–5 not only illustrate his conscious rejection of classicism: they also were his means of rejection. There was always a strain of humour in his make-up—it had shown already in the scurrilous sketches with which he defaced his otherwise praiseworthy geometry exercise books; in a 'humorous sketchbook' to which he referred in 1899; in much of his writing and very frequently in his mature work. His unleashing of it in his etchings inevitably disturbed the harmony essential to classicism, and helped him to deviate from naturalism, to concern himself with individuality of style, to return to the world of fantasy on which he had only recently turned his back, and generally to challenge in himself the intellectual control and the love of beauty which, he felt, stood between him and the mature artistic personality he was eager to achieve. Beauty, he decided, he could serve 'through its enemies' (J 142; 1902); serving beauty directly without fear of banality could come later. In 1903 he declared war on his own intellectualism: 'You shall pray: Give oblivion to my spirit that it may wander' (J 700; 1905). Later, in his writing and teaching, he was to describe more than once the synthesis of conscious control and intuitive action out of which creative work may arise. For the present, circumstances seem to have been in his favour. He was living with his family in Berne and so suffering no material hardship, but he was gradually moving away from his father who had once seemed to him an unequalled source of wisdom. This fact, and the stodginess of the Swiss bourgeoisie around him, supplied him with material and kept sharp the edge of his satire. At the same time he was becoming familiar with realms of artistic expression he had not known before: Beardsley, Blake, Félicien Rops and, above all, Goya, helped him through their example. Klee's etchings of 1903–5 are technically very accomplished and stylistically original; they may owe a good deal to Goya and to others as much in the way the bitterness of the content is carried and in the way it is drawn as in the subject itself, but none of them could even loosely be described as exercises in anybody else's manner. Many etchings other than those known were attempted and destroyed, or conceived and left unexecuted.

Meanwhile Klee drew, did 'that little bit of painting' (J 558; 1904), and began to make some effort to find a public. It was perhaps easier in Central Europe and in that decade to have graphic work treated seriously by journals and galleries than it is now, but Klee met with little interest. None of his work was shown until 1906 when through Stuck's support the Munich Sezession jury accepted ten etchings mounted together in one frame. His reading, always voluminous and wide-ranging, seems to have been particularly energetic in this period. He saw a good deal of art in the municipal galleries of Switzerland. He also wrote theatre and concert reviews for a Swiss paper and took on two private pupils, one for the violin and one for painting.

1905 saw a decisive step forward. 'I shall have to be relatively satisfied with my etchings, but I am not a specialist and cannot go on in this way' (J 632; 1905). He must search for the logical way out of this position and thinks he may have found it in scratching with an etching needle on a blackened glass plate: 'The means here are no longer the black line but the white. The ground is not daylight but night; that energy should illuminate corresponds to the processes of nature. This surely represents a transition from graphic work to painting' (J 632; 1905). He had actually experimented with working on glass as early as September 1902, when he scratched lines through a coating of asphalt on glass and made a photographic print from it. But now he becomes fascinated with light and with the accurate control of tonal gradations. His etchings, he says, are Opus 1; now he feels ready for Opus 2.

In May-June 1905 he spent a fortnight in Paris on a pretty exhaustive study of the paintings in the Louvre and the Luxembourg and of painted decorations in such monuments as the Panthéon. He was interested by what he saw of the work of Manet, Monet, Sisley, Renoir and Pissarro. Carrière he noted as a good guide in matters of tone. But what really impressed him were Corot (whom he already admired in Geneva), Watteau, the late Rembrandt and Goya. There is no indication that he saw anything of Fauvism which was about to burst upon the Paris scene at that year's Salon d'Automne, nor that he knew anything of Post-Impressionism except in so far as the paintings of Hodler and of Cuno Amiet, seen in Munich and Switzerland, can come under that heading. Having seen bright colour in them, and having experienced Central European versions of Impressionism, he was not at all taken aback by his first contact with the French Impressionists. Indeed, Impressionism, for so many late nineteenth-century and early twentieth-century painters a gateway to modernism, was to Klee one aspect of the tradition of naturalism: naturalism with light colours under the control of tone.

Through the mediation of certain friends, Klee in 1905 was in touch with Germany's other main art centre, Berlin—in touch, that is, with publishers and writers. His problem was the familiar one: his work was too unconventional for anyone to risk showing or publishing it without the support of an established reputation, yet how could Klee achieve this reputation without having his work seen? Trying to break through this barrier Klee visited Berlin. He saw there exhibitions and art collections and called on a writer with whom he had previously corresponded, Professor Heilblut, without any success except that Heilblut gave him a book on Goya. He returned to Berne via Kassel and its splendid Rembrandts, and Karlsruhe and its famous Grünewald *Crucifixion*.

The business of making money and establishing a reputation had become more important to him: Paul Klee and Lily Stumpf, after four years' engagement, were married on September 15, 1906. They settled in a flat in Munich. Klee had been eager for some time to move out of Switzerland; in Munich, 'the city of five thousand painters' (J 780; 1906), of galleries, operas, theatres and concerts, they would be able to live, build up congenial relationships, and work—Lily out of the house most of the day, giving piano lessons, he at home, drawing and painting and preparing subtle meals. Moreover, he had his ten etchings in the Sezession exhibition, and this gave him hope. Actually, when he submitted some glass paintings to the 1907 Spring Sezession jury they were all rejected, and that year Klee did not show any of his work. On November 30, 1907, he became a father, a little reluctantly. Once Felix had been born Klee soon found himself fascinated by the growth and development of the child and there is plenty of evidence of a warm relationship between them.

He continued drawing and painting on glass. He developed a technique whereby he coated the plate with white tempera instead of asphalt, drew his lines through that and then added tonal patches of black or grey on the back. Although he was still far from being the painter he wished to become, he continually gained ground in the form of permanently valuable insight into artistic creation and the problems of pictorial art. 'The practised hand often knows much better than the head' (J 760; 1906). 'Like man himself, a painting has a skeleton, muscles and skin. It is possible to speak of a particular pictorial anatomy' (J 844; 1908). 'To achieve vital harmony in a picture it must be constructed out of parts in themselves incomplete, brought into harmony only at the last stroke' (J 844; 1908). 'I have got to the point where I can translate "Nature" directly into my own style. I have gone beyond the concept of "studies". Now everything will be Klee, whether days or only moments come between experience and response... Shall I ever get this far in the field of colour?' (J 757; 1906). A friend introduced him to the art of Daumier and Ensor and so further widened Klee's experience of art. From the same source he got van Gogh's letters, the story of another painter's struggle towards colour, achieved through observation of colour in the work of others and by going south into a climate where colour dominates sensation at the expense of tone. In 1908, when the Munich public were for the first time able to see work by such men as Bonnard, Vuillard and Valotton at the Spring Sezession, there were also two van Gogh exhibitions, one very large, the other smaller but including many of the more famous works. Partly as a result of these experiences, Klee that year planned an intense campaign of oil painting, in three directions (J 824 and 827; 1908). He would do figure paintings from nature (a) by establishing first the environment or space and then, on another occasion, painting the figure itself, ultimately realising a proper interaction between the two (all to be done with the palette knife to keep the colours clean), and (b) putting down local colours in broad areas and then modelling with lighter or darker tones. He would also (c) do another kind of oil painting: he would put down patches of colour in freely invented complexes, straight out of the sensation of the moment, as the irradicable essence of the picture; these he would then study, like in childhood he studied the marble table-tops in his uncle's restaurant, to find suggestions of figurative content to be picked out by tonal emphasis.

These plans reveal with striking clarity the problems confronting the intelligent young painter of that period. Two years later Kandinsky was to accept 'freely invented complexes' as self-sufficient, while other painters, such as Delaunay, found themselves in positions very much like Klee's. All the fundamental concepts of modern painting existed, but they existed in a tangled skein of ideas more easily unravelled by us to-day than at the time. Unravelling them meant discarding ideals and skills that were highly valued and had been achieved with effort: in Klee's case his particular skill in recording tone. Writing in 1908 he sounds first like an action painter but ends up with Leonardo da Vinci's wall, yet in February of that year he had noted what, one would have thought, was the essential discovery necessary to make him into the colourist he wanted to be: 'I have learned to distinguish tonal painting (with or without colour) from colour painting. Got it!' (J 811; 1908). In the event it took another six years for the painter Klee to be born. A number of experiences helped him on his way.

In January 1909 he saw a large Marées exhibition in Munich. He had seen Marées' frescoes in Naples in 1902 and had been impressed by them. Marées (1837–1887), emerging out of a very confused artistic climate, had struggled towards an integration of monumental form, simplified naturalism and constructive colour with such seriousness that his mature work warrants comparison with Cézanne. Later the same year 'I saw eight paintings by Cézanne at the Sezession. There is my teacher *par excellence*, much more a teacher than van Gogh' (J 857; 1909). Also in 1909 he saw an exhibition of Matisse at the Thannhauser Gallery in Munich.

1910 was a particularly eventful year. His first one-man show opened in August at the Berne Museum and then transferred to Basel, Winterthur and Zürich: 56 items (including one consisting of six sketches) done between 1907 and 1910, mostly chalk, pencil or pen drawings, one etching, one glass painting and a few watercolours. He received a favourable notice and sold a few works, but it was hardly a triumph. More encouraging was a letter received from Alfred Kubin, a graphic artist two years older than Klee, then making a name for himself as a specialist in horrific book illustrations. Kubin wanted to own a Klee and subsequently selected one out of a handful sent him. In January 1911 he visited Klee in Munich. They looked at Klee's work: 'He seemed so enthusiastic that he pulled me along with him. We sat absolutely enraptured before my drawings!' (J 888; 1911).

When in the spring of 1910 he tried to assess the progress he had made he recognised that 'I still am not capable of painting, in spite of my strict observation of tonal values and in spite of my clever way of matching accurately the gradations from light to dark' (J 872). Yet a few days later he wrote: 'And now a revolutionary discovery: more important than nature and the study of nature is one's attitude to the contents of one's paint-box. One day I shall have to be capable of improvising freely on the colour keyboard of my row of watercolour pots' (J 873). In April 1910 he announced to himself a New offensive against the citadel of painting. First a general ground of white thinned with linseed oil. Then lightly colour the whole field with large patches of various colours which should run together and remain free of any tonal function. Third, the drawing, independent and substituting for tonal modulation. Then, finally, a few bass notes to prevent softening, and I mean notes not too dark but colour notes…

The purity of means: either tonal values in proportion as such, or: as substitute for the missing tonal value, line (as frontier between different tone values) or contrast of colour values. Because in art everything is best said only once, and always in the simplest possible way (J 875–876).

In June, with a painstaking thoroughness that reveals the effort involved in clarifying his intentions, he enlarged on the subject:

I shall transfer the shadow organisation, the step by step application of light and dark tones, to colour so that each step (and the number of steps is to be reduced to the minimum) each step in tone value corresponds to a colour; in other words I shall not lighten a colour with white or darken it with black, but always use one colour for one step. For the next step the next colour (J 879).

There follows the first oil painting of Klee's maturity, *Girl with jugs* (plate 3).

Klee's progress towards mastery of colour did not involve any loss of interest in the graphic media. Through years of work, alternating between strict drawing from nature and imaginative drawing, he had been able to fashion line into a physical extension of his spirit, leaving a visible trace of his emotions. At times he stimulated his fantasy by starting from a few accidentally scribbled lines, developing them according to the figurative hints they held. He feared a tendency for his drawing to become shallow and decorative, but found that energetic drawing from nature offered a corrective. As early as 1908 he realised that he had here a precious and highly individualised means of expression; perhaps his growing tendency to exclude line from his painting encouraged him at this time to assess its independent function.

Having recently gained strength from naturalistic studies, I can again venture into my deepest region (Urgebiet) of psychical improvisation. Here, linked only very indirectly to any visual impression, I can again dare to give form to whatever weighs on my spirit. To note experiences which could translate themselves into line even in absolute darkness... In this way my genuine personality will be able to speak out and to liberate itself with the utmost freedom (J 842).

The years around 1910–1912 were very fruitful ones for Klee the graphic artist as well as for Klee the nascent painter. 1911 saw the realisation of an undertaking he had conceived two years earlier: he illustrated Voltaire's *Candide*. One would have guessed that this was a book that would appeal to him; in fact in January 1906 he had written in his diary: 'I have been reading, indeed reading a unique book: Candide by Voltaire. Three exclamation marks!' (J 743). He did not actually tackle the illustrations until five years later, when he found the task interesting enough to lift him out of a mood of despondency. He did twenty-six drawings for the book. In spite of the good offices of enthusiastic friends, the illustrated book was not published until 1920; an English edition was published by Pantheon Books, New York, in 1944.

1911 was also the year in which Klee came into contact with the newly formed *Blaue Reiter* group in Munich. He met Marc, Macke, Jawlensky, Gabriele Münter and Marianne von Werefkin, and renewed and deepened the acquaintanceship he had had with Kandinsky during his period with Stuck. Through his involvement with the group (he contributed to the second *Blaue Reiter* exhibition in 1912), Klee also became more familiar with the work of artists in foreign countries. Not only were several foreigners members of the group or closely associated with it, particularly Russians, but the first exhibition put on by the group (December 1911) included work by Delaunay and

Rousseau, while the second (graphic work only, March 1912) included Picasso, Derain, Braque, Vlaminck and Malevich. Unlike the *Brücke* group founded in Dresden in 1905 with its emphasis on social protest through pictorial violence, *Der Blaue Reiter* supported all serious attempts to create new artistic languages. It did not propose a style, only a general faith in the power of painting to communicate, principally through colour, those stirrings of the human spirit to which in the past only music had been free to do justice. The first world war killed the group by dispersing its members and by claiming Marc and Macke as victims, but Klee benefited from its brief existence in many ways, not least from the knowledge that he was no longer isolated.

In April 1912 Klee visited Paris for the second time. He again spent part of his sixteen days there in the Louvre and the Luxembourg, but this time he also sought out modern artists and their work. He visited the German journalist and collector Wilhelm Uhde, and saw in his flat paintings by Picasso, Braque and Rousseau. He went to Kahnweiler's gallery and saw work by Picasso, Derain and Vlaminck, to Bernheim-jeune's and saw work by Matisse. Most important, on April 11: 'In the morning I visited Delaunay in his studio' (J 910). The journal does not say anything else about this meeting, but we may assume that the two artists took to each other, since later in the year Delaunay sent Klee an article on light and colour which Klee translated and which was published in the Berlin magazine *Der Sturm* in January 1913. In his paintings at this time Delaunay was moving from the geometrically abstracted townscapes of his *Window* series to the completely abstract colour rhythms and harmonies of his *Disks*. He exerted considerable influence on *Blaue Reiter* members—in fact Delaunay's work was more appreciated and better known in Germany than in Paris—and Klee too was affected by him, though perhaps in a less obvious manner: Delaunay confirmed the expressive, as Cézanne had shown the constructive, power of colour, but Klee's *Girl with jugs* (1910) proves that he had himself gone a long way in this direction.

Perhaps the most important year in Klee's development was 1914. For years, as has been seen, he had been preparing himself to paint, to be a painter principally and a graphic artist secondarily, through experiments in and attempts at painting, through studying the paintings of others, and through constructive thought about the essential qualities of painting. By now his understanding was profound, his technical ability was considerable, and in the graphic field he had achieved a gratifying completeness of control and expression. But as a painter he had produced little when the year began. By the end of the year he had produced not only an outstanding series of watercolours but also some fine oil paintings, such as *Homage to Picasso* (plate 7). If Klee's graduation as painter can be given a date then that date must be 1914, the year of his visit to North Africa.

Van Gogh, who wrote to his brother that 'the colours of the prism are veiled in the mists of the North', had gone south to Arles in 1888 to immerse himself in Mediterranean colour. Fifty-six years earlier Delacroix had gone to Morocco to experience a great deepening of his awareness and knowledge of colour. Whether Klee planned his trip as a means of propelling himself head first into the world of painting is uncertain. What

Two men meet, each believing the other to be of superior social standing

Group of sculptures: heads and figures

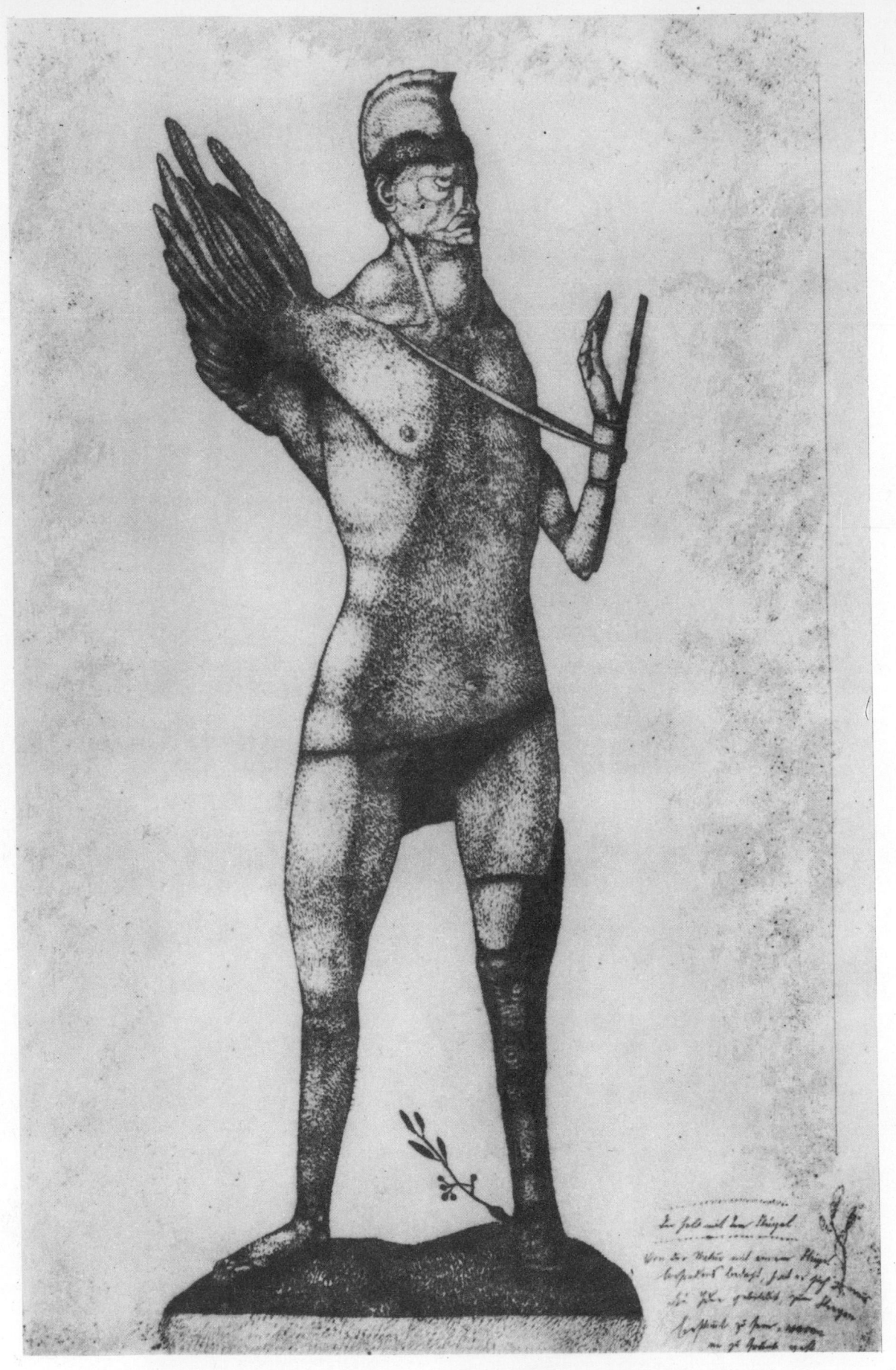

Hero with a wing

is certain is that the trip was his idea and that he proposed it to two painter friends, Louis Moilliet, whom he had known since childhood, and August Macke, whom he had come to know comparatively recently through *Blaue Reiter* activities. Marseilles was decided on as their meeting place. They gathered there on April 5, set out for Tunis on April 6 and arrived there on April 7. They divided their time between Tunis, its suburb Saint-Germain, Hamamet and Kairouan. Klee began the journey home by himself on April 19, travelling back through Italy and arriving in Munich on April 25.

During his days in North Africa he did a great deal of work. Almost daily his journal speaks of the watercolours he is doing. On his first day in Tunis he attacked the problem of what he describes as the 'urban-architecture/picture-architecture synthesis'. He also attempted paintings and saw with equanimity that he still failed to achieve what he wished for: 'I am not at all depressed over this. There is no point in hurrying when one wants so much' (J 926k). Much more important to him than his paintings were the visual and mental impressions he was gathering. Already in Marseilles he had noted a colour scale new to him. As the ship took them past Sardinia he noticed a growing intensity of colour. Arrived in Africa he was struck by the rhythmic quality of the cubic white houses of the first Arabian town he saw and by the remarkable clarity of the colours. Above all he sensed a fairy-tale quality in the life and landscape of Tunisia that moved him profoundly, a strange actuality of fabulousness that seemed at once distant and yet clearly rooted in the physical environment: 'Matter and dream at one and the same time and, as a third element utterly subject to them, myself' (J 926e). Only gradually did he feel himself able to transmit these unfamiliar qualities through his watercolours. The first attempts were too European ('I could have done it in Marseilles'), but ultimately he managed to satisfy himself, producing watercolours, in which he considerably transformed the subject while fully retaining its objective character. There came a moment, on April 16, when he felt he was saturated by his experience and he wrote these often quoted lines:

> I stop working now. My experiences press into me so deeply and so gently; I can feel it, and thus am assured, without effort. Colour has taken possession of me. I don't have to strain after it any more. Colour has conquered me for always. I know that. That is the meaning of this fortunate hour: I and colour are one. I am a painter. (J 926 o).

He did do some more paintings and watercolours during the next days, but he felt that these were insignificant beside what was going on inside him. 'I feel a certain restlessness: my cart is overloaded and I must get down to work' (J 926r). During his swift journey home he noticed little beyond the changing character of the Italian landscape.

The first world war broke out in August and the art circle Klee had known in Munich disintegrated. Kandinsky, Jawlensky and Gabriele Münter left Germany; August Macke was killed at the front during the first weeks of the war; Franz Marc, to whom Klee felt particularly drawn, was killed in 1916. Although Klee thought of himself as a German, and although he was deeply affected by the deaths of his friends, the war was to him an external event that in no way related to his artistic life. He did say, echoing the art historian Worringer, that 'the more fearful this world becomes, as at this moment, the more art becomes abstract' (J 953; 1915), and he produced abstract paintings as though to prove the statement, but he also felt that his own inner struggles had prepared him for the war.

He was called up in 1916 and found himself doing administrative work, also painting aeroplanes and delivering them. It was obviously not an ideal life for a creative artist but he accepted it in good spirit and found some pleasures in it. He managed to do his own work, often in rooms rented near his post or even while on duty by such devices as doing it in an open drawer in case of discovery (J 1090; 1917). He wondered, in fact, whether the tensions and obstacles of these years might not have advanced him as an artist, and certainly the watercolour *Once emerged from the grey of night* (plate 10, 1918) shows his fully matured manner and could have been done ten years later.

Materially the war years were for him a period of growing success. Herwarth Walden, owner of the *Der Sturm* gallery in Berlin and publisher of the *Der Sturm* magazine, showed Klee's work, sold some of it, bought some for himself, and published some. Other writers and publishers took an interest in Klee, wrote about him and reproduced examples of his work. Two books on him came out in 1920, as well as the illustrated edition of *Candide*. These years of relative seclusion and restriction encouraged Klee to think even more deeply about the creative process, about the means of art and about his own artistic personality, and he began to write down some of his thoughts in a more communicable form than he had used in his journal. The outcome was the *Creative Credo* which he contributed to an anthology of artists' statements published under that title in 1920, and which summarises his ideas on the relationship of art to nature and presents his thoughts on graphic art (his reputation was still primarily that of a graphic artist). The statement he made in this book is prepared for in many journal entries during the preceding years, such as: 'Everything ephemeral is no more than a parable. All we see is a proposition, a possibility, a makeshift. True reality as yet lies much deeper, invisible' (J 1081; 1917); and: 'In art it is not seeing that is so important but making visible' (J 1134; 1918).

In December 1918 Klee went home to Munich on leave and managed to get himself demobilised — and at this point his journal ends.

The remainder of the story of Klee's life may be told more briefly. As an artist he was now fully mature. His work during the following twenty-two years covers an unbelievably large range without ever being cast adrift from the anchor of his own personality. It is unusually difficult to find influences from movements or from individual artists in his work and it is impossible to show any convincing line of development. It was his habit to work on several pictures at one time, so that not only one year but even one day would find him producing work of bewildering variety. During the last three or four years of his life there would seem to be evidence of a degree of stylistic concentration in his work, both in his paintings and in his drawings, yet the last painting he completed, now known as the *Still life on a dark ground* suggests an entirely new departure.

His material position was an increasingly comfortable one, partly through the growing interest in his work and partly because he accepted teaching positions which brought

Munich, the main station

him a secure income and at the same time left him a good deal of free time. He never lived extravagantly.

In 1919 the senior students of the Stuttgart art academy, led by Schlemmer, tried to persuade and push the authorities into inviting Klee to fill the post recently vacated by Adolf Hölzel. Schlemmer, soon to be Klee's colleague in another school, appears to have had a remarkable understanding of Klee's work. He wrote to a friend that 'there is in Klee a piety and deep insight which leads him to play in a childlike way' (letter to Meyer, February 23, 1919). The governors of the academy, who had promised the students a 'modern' teacher, turned down the Klee proposal in the face of considerable student agitation, saying that 'after searching examination of the earlier and more recent works of Mr Klee it was found that they bore a frivolous character and did not give evidence of the strong will towards structure and pictorial organisation at present rightly demanded by the youngest artists' (letter to Meyer, December 28, 1919).

In 1920 Klee was invited to join the staff of the Bauhaus in Weimar by its director, the architect Walter Gropius. Founded in 1919, at a time, that is, when Germany was in a state of material collapse and social confusion, the Bauhaus was created to unite the arts through emphasis on their common roots in design and the crafts and through the promulgation of egalitarian feelings that hovered somewhere between medievalist romanticism and expressionist socialism. Its first years were very difficult. Short of funds, continuously attacked by reactionary forces in Weimar, confused in its intentions and wasting some of its energies on internal disruptions, the Bauhaus was nevertheless the most adventurous essay in modern education for art and design undertaken anywhere, and gradually it transformed itself into the industrialised institution it became famous as. Meanwhile Gropius, slowly freeing himself from the ties that linked the Bauhaus to the older art and design schools it replaced in Weimar, gathered together an unequalled team of teachers. He had opened with the painters Feininger and Itten and the sculptor Marcks, and soon he added other painters, including Schlemmer, Klee and Kandinsky.

Klee accepted Gropius's warm invitation (warmer than the occasion demanded, in view of the fact that some members of the Bauhaus, like the gentlemen of Stuttgart, suspected Klee of artistic frivolity), and was officially appointed to the staff in November 1920. He arrived in Weimar in January 1921. He taught in the school for ten years, moving (after some hesitation) with the Bauhaus to Dessau in July 1926. During the years 1923–5 the Bauhaus, led by Gropius but following the path compellingly indicated by Moholy-Nagy, was converted from its expressionist idealistic aims into a rationalistic institution priding itself on its functionalist attitude to design, in which the fine arts played a minor role if any role at all. In 1921 Klee wrote a memorandum to Gropius, presumably in answer to an enquiry, stating his attitude to the oppositions within the Bauhaus in characteristic terms:

> I welcome the fact that so variously directed forces should work together at our Bauhaus. I consider valuable also the struggle between these forces as long as the outcome expresses itself in what is achieved... Altogether there is nothing that is right or wrong, but rather everything lives and develops through the play of forces, as also in the whole world good and evil in the long run productively co-operate. (H. M. Wingler, *Das Bauhaus*, Bramsche 1962.)

Nevertheless he could not but regret the transformation of the Bauhaus, involving as it did his displacement from a more or less central position to the periphery. At the same time the influence of his personality seems to have been noticeable even during the most decidedly anti-art years of the Bauhaus (the directorship of Hannes Meyer, 1928–30). Max Bill, who studied at the Bauhaus during 1927–9, has written that 'Klee seemed to offer a compensation for the rationalistic attitude of the Bauhaus students', and other former Bauhaus students and staff have spoken of Klee's effectiveness as an unaligned element in a school often divided into factions and as a quiet, creative spirit in an institution that sometimes allowed itself to be dominated by brief enthusiasms and by technique. Klee taught as design instructor *(Formmeister)* in the stained glass and weaving workshops, but more important than this were his lecture courses investigating the functional potentialities of form and colour, and the voluntary painting classes which he gave for those who were interested enough to come, which, as the Bauhaus became more technology-centred, played an increasingly significant role by encouraging anti-authoritarian attitudes. Kandinsky too gave such classes, but Max Bill has reported that Klee's were much better attended.

In 1931 Klee left the Bauhaus to become visiting professor at the Düsseldorf Academy. For political reasons the Bauhaus was now in very troubled waters, whereas Düsseldorf offered a position involving less teaching and less conflict. In 1933 Klee was forced to resign by the now triumphant Nazis — not being a Jew he was considered guilty of 'culture-bolshevism' — and the Klees left Germany for Berne.

There Klee died in 1940, on June 29, at the age of sixty. He had been increasingly ill during the last four to five years, but rather than showing any decline in the quantity or value of his artistic production, these years demonstrate a remarkable efflorescence in his art — high summer rather than fall. The paintings of his last years are often larger than before, and stylistically they and the drawings contemporary with them suggest a new toughness and a new dramatic energy, so that many well-informed friends of Klee, who had long delighted in his more delicate, often more whimsical works, found themselves nonplussed. To us, many of them seem not only to come among the finest works of his whole, enormously fruitful career, but also in several respects to herald, in the centre of war-ridden Europe, artistic adventures shortly to be undertaken by a younger generation in the New World.

KLEE AND THE CREATIVE UNCONSCIOUS

'. . . in experience, the poet begins entirely with the unconscious . . . and poetry, it seems to me, consists precisely in being able to express and communicate that unconscious — i.e. to carry it over into an object.'

These words were written by the German poet and dramatist Schiller in a letter to Goethe, 1801. He was commenting on Schelling's book, *System of Transcendental Idealism* (1800), in which it was argued that art is the product of the interaction of, on the one hand, 'intelligence', 'conscious' and 'freedom', and, on the other, 'nature', 'unconscious' and 'necessity'. Goethe replied to Schiller in even more emphatic terms:
'I believe that everything that the genius does as genius eventuates in the unconscious'. Jean Paul (J.P.F. Richter), a particularly popular author among the Expressionist generation, wrote in 1804 of the unconscious as 'the mightiest element in the poet', related it to instinct in animals, and characterised it as the dark abyss from which man draws his dreams and demons. In short, at least a partial understanding of the role of the unconscious in artistic creation existed in the German literary world of around 1800. (See: M.H. Abrams, *The Mirror and the Lamp*, London 1960; page 209 *et seq.*)
Klee's generation was profoundly interested in the writings of German Romanticism and so it is not surprising that, although he is fully aware of the unconscious, and perhaps more than any other painter of his time worked in such a way as to give every opportunity for it to contribute decisively, there is no mention in his published writings of the modern creators of psychology. Klee inherited the concept of the unconscious as part of the German cultural tradition. The following quotations are intended to illustrate his awareness of this function and his attitude to it:
Paintings come into existence without conscious control; sometimes also with conscious control. You don't know exactly what they are going to be like. Perhaps you want them to turn out like this or like that. In any case the best pictures cannot be willed; they just come into being (MK 28).
The painter, when he is really a painter, forms — or rather: he allows form to arise. He has no intention, no direct one. He is glad to contribute something to the self-forming work, this or that, adding an accent to accents, directions to direction, in order to articulate, clarify, order, to stress, emphasise, reduce in order to strengthen,

activate, suppress. He knows a great deal, but he only knows it *afterwards* (EPK 87; conversation 1930).

Let action be extraordinary and not according to rule (J 832; 1908).

KLEE AND ORGANIC CREATION IN ART

Klee had a profound understanding of the organic nature of art and artistic production. A corollary, though not a necessary one, of the concept of the unconscious as the creative source, the idea of organic form in art achieved by a process analogous to natural growth was also first propounded by the German Romantic literary theorists, and most clearly by Schlegel who wrote of art 'creating autonomously like nature'. Werner Haftmann (in *The Inward Vision*, London 1958; page 15) has described Klee's working process most coherently:

Klee's procedure is entirely new. He does not start from pre-formed visual images of nature, he starts from the picture itself. Summoned to action at the moment of inspiration, he begins without any conscious, let alone object-directed, intention. Entirely

The great dome

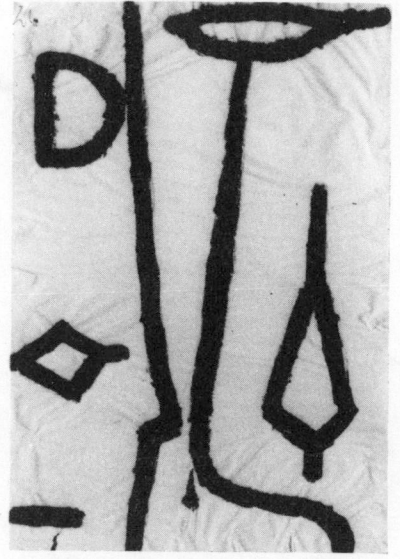

Injured   *Portrait of an expressionist*

engrossed in his work, thinking only of organisation, he articulates, orders, and moves his pictorial planes, and, intensely meditating on the emerging world of forms, follows up every lead suggested by the developing design. The subtly organised patterns grow slowly out of the chaotic background, and, as one layer of colour succeeds another, the picture gradually acquires its broad melodic outline and evocative richness.

One should add that at this stage, in producing some of his works, Klee accepts the evocative content of the images that have arisen, emphasises it, and thus gives the work a 'subject'. The title of the picture, often added long after completion, can then confirm, contradict or enlarge its apparent meaning.

Klee repeatedly stressed the importance of the creative *process* and believed that it is ultimately the process which is communicated. Something of this is already implied in the programme he set himself in June 1902, shortly after his return from Italy:

Then I shall make something modest, invent for myself some very small formal motif. My pencil will be able to hold it, without technique. One favourable moment will be enough; the little motif is easily, briefly put down. And already it is done! It was a tiny, but a real act, and one day a work will grow out of the repetition of small, personal acts on which I shall be able to build.

Eighteen years later he reinforced this statement in the *Creative Credo:*

Does a picture come into being at one stroke? No, it is constructed bit by bit, like a house. The work of art is above all a process of creation; it is never experienced as a mere product.

Every time that in my work an image leaves the stage of genesis and I approach my goal, intensity very quickly diminishes and I have to seek new avenues. In working, the way is the essential thing, and becoming is more important than being (J 926u; 1924).

You will never achieve anything unless you work up towards it. You cannot break in halfway through the process and least of all can you start with a result. You must start at the beginning. Then you will avoid all trace of artificiality and the creative process will function without interruption (1923, to Bauhaus students; quoted by Werner Haftmann in *Mind and work of Paul Klee*, London 1954).

I have never concerned myself with other painters but have just worked, let everything grow (MK 59).

Creation as formal movement is the essential element in the work. At the beginning the motif, the plugging in of energy, sperm (J 943; 1944).

Creation lives as genesis behind the visible surface of the work. Looking into the past all intelligent people can see that; looking forwards — into the future — only the creative (J 932; 1914).

KLEE AND NATURE

It is no longer necessary to spend time on demolishing the old claim that abstract art necessarily involves an aversion from or opposition to nature. This in itself may be due to the ever-growing interest in Klee, whose involvement in nature was as deep as that of any naturalistic painter and whose refusal to recognise any kind of barrier between figurative and abstract art foreshadowed the endeavours of many living artists to find a synthesis of the two fields. The evidence for Klee's interest in nature — or, to put it more pointedly, for his need to base himself and his art on a close relationship to nature — is plentiful in his works and in his writing and teaching. His journal is full of references to working out of doors, to observation of nature, to nature's richness and variety, and even to the danger of leaning too heavily on nature which can become 'a comfortable crutch' (J 536; 1903). Visitors to Klee's studios record his collection of bits and pieces of nature; Felix Klee describes his father's affectionate familiarity with nature. Many of the quotations already given relate to this theme.

Speaking in 1930 to Hans-Friedrich Geist, painter and art master in a village school, Klee said:

Nature, if we love her, will ultimately lead us into liberty. Of course the painter must study nature. You know it! Do it. It is more sensible than poetising or borrowing from the primitives. Follow the natural paths of creation, the genesis and functions of forms. That is the best school. Through nature you will perhaps achieve your own configurations and, one day, be nature yourself, creating like nature (EPK 91).

Klee and his family seem to have made frequent excursions into the country from their homes in Germany and from his parents' house in Berne. Speaking to his Düsseldorf students he referred to some such occasion probably long before:

At one time I had been working exclusively at home for weeks, when suddenly I discovered, one day on a walk near Berne, how really extraordinarily beautiful nature is. I tried to hold on to this feeling. To this day I always make studies out of doors, without directly sketching (the eye itself makes the sketch), and there are places that influence me profoundly. Without studies from nature we cannot make progress anywhere (MK 13).

He valued his genetic process of creation as an essentially natural method, and its outcome as 'allegorically related to nature' *(Creative Credo)*.

KLEE AND PRIMITIVE ART

The close relationship of some of Klee's work to the art of primitives, children and mental defectives, has long been noted. At first, indeed, the relationship was pointed out in order to disparage him. He himself was aware of the connection and certainly had great respect for what we may loosely call primitive art. His reliance on the contribution of the unconscious in his own work, and his interest in the creative process generally, drew him to study the relatively untrammelled transmission of subconscious urges in such art.

Ellen Marsh has studied the relationship of Klee's work to that of children:

The child forms his image quite naturally, drawing from both within—the inner eye or imagination—or without—the outer eye or world of nature. His representation of this image in the material is direct, and, although the aesthetic selections he makes may be as difficult for him as are the adult artist's for him, they are, in the main, forced out by an inner certainty or necessity and not by outside logic or influence. It is this inner certainty that Klee wants to attain. ('Paul Klee and the art of children', in *College Art Journal*, New York, winter 1957).

Klee admitted to his colleague Lothar Schreyer that he sometimes failed to achieve this directness:

Child's play! Those gentlemen the critics often say that my pictures resemble the scribbles and messes of children. I hope they do! The pictures that my little boy Felix paints are often better than mine, because mine have often been filtered through the brain, which regrettably I cannot always avoid because sometimes I work too much. We must serve honestly and loyally the shift of consciousness that our generation has experienced and experiences. You just as I and all of us here. I often say this, and sometimes it is not taken seriously enough, that worlds have opened themselves to us, and continue to open themselves, which also belong to nature but into which not all men look, perhaps really only children, the insane and the primitive... And what they see is to me the most precious confirmation (ESB 168 *et seq.*).

To Geist, the art master, Klee spoke of the dangers both of borrowing motifs from child art and of forcing one's own ideas on the children:

The child wants to go forward, to move on; he does not want to linger on the first steps. Pure naïvety is lost, and must be lost. Consciousness demands its rights (today more than ever) so thoroughly that the child merely records and that knowledge gradually supplants creation. How much does not a sixteen-year-old know about trees, ships and aeroplanes? He is not capable of translating so much knowledge into forms. Must he then, should he by chance be an artist, forego artistic creation? (EPK 92).

For the teen-age child he recommended a close study of nature. Since he considered this an essential basis for himself and for adult students it is fair to say that he did not distinguish fundamentally between the adolescent and the adult in this matter:

> When the demand arises, lead your pupils to nature, into nature. Let them experience how a bud forms, how a tree grows, how a butterfly opens its wings, so that they may become as rich, as mobile, as wilful as nature. Contemplation is revelation; contemplation is insight into God's workshop. There, in the lap of nature, lies the secret of creation (EPK 91).

KLEE ON SIMPLICITY

No one would consider Klee's work as distinguishable by its simplicity; at the same time it is clear that many a complex picture originated in a simple element (the 'small, personal acts on which I shall be able to build'), and that he attached great importance to the simplicity of pictorial means:

> Reduction! One wants to say more than nature and makes the impossible error of wanting to say it with more means than she, instead of with fewer (J 834; 1908).
>
> Nature can permit herself extravagance in all things; the artist must be economical to the last degree (J 857; 1909).

It was his own disciplined simplicity, based on professional experience, that gave (Klee said) his work its primitive character.

> In simplicity too there can be riches. This should give us the courage to be simple...
> To create much spiritually out of little (MK 37).

One is reminded of the words of another creative genius in another sphere, the architect Mies van der Rohe (who has a fine collection of Klees): 'Less is more.'

KLEE AND COLOUR

In the introduction emphasis has been placed on Klee's innate sensibility to colour and on his slow struggle towards the point at which his colour sensations and his capacity to find visual expression for them met. The importance of colour in his mature work is self-evident. Indeed, it may be said that, while much of it rests on the twin supports of his gifts as a colourist and as graphic artist, colour, from 1914 on, is almost always the principal element. One is tempted to add that Klee was the greatest colourist of his age; more prudently it may be said that there was only one other painter for whom, as for Klee, colour was so inextricably both the essential constructive factor and the chief vehicle for expression, and that was Matisse.

The last section of the lecture notes published as *The Thinking Eye* (London 1961) is devoted to Klee's instruction in colour. This, taken in conjunction with the notes on this section in the book's appendix, gives a fairly complete picture of his communicable thoughts about colour. His resistance to colour theories is typical of him; the more comprehensive the theory the more abhorrent it was to him. At the same time it is clear that he had given time to the most important theories, and the one he recommends is that of the German Romantic painter, Phillipp Otto Runge (1777–1810). In the year of his death Runge published in Hamburg a *Colour Sphere, or construction showing the relationships of all the colours to one another and their complete affinity. Together with an essay on the significance of colours in nature by Henrik Steffens.* It is interesting that Klee should have turned to the Romantic period for the colour theory that offends him least, though not surprising when one remembers his generation's interest in the art and thought of German Romanticism. But the close relationship between Runge and the naturalist and geologist Steffens must have pleased Klee with his insistence on art's basis in nature, and he probably approved of Runge's often poetic, sometimes mystical, attitude to colour.

To both Runge and Klee, colour was the irrational element in painting:

Colour has always got something mysterious about it that cannot be properly understood... Colours are the most irrational element in painting. They have something suggestive about them, a suggestive power... The old masters placed colour as the last part into their pictorial constructions. We want to be colourists first and foremost (MK 19).

Although colour theories inevitably base themselves on the colours of the spectrum as absolutes, Klee goes on, we can really only experience what we as painters consider the true red, blue or yellow, psychically. So it is not surprising to find that his colour instruction does not include statements on what is and what is not good colour, nor relate particularly closely to his own work. Even more than when he spoke of form Klee approached colour tentatively, indicating possibilities for investigation rather than issuing directions. As he said to his Düsseldorf students:

How colours are used, how light and dark are employed, depends on the individual (MK 21).

KLEE IN HIS STUDIO

During the years in Munich until he was called up in 1916, married to Lily and the father of Felix, Klee had to use the kitchen of their flat as his studio. Since he also filled the role of housewife and cook this may have worked better than it normally would, especially as he seems to have considered cooking a fine art, too. From the cast-iron balcony he could look down on children playing below in the Hohenzollernstrasse, and observe the townscape beyond. Some of his drawings and glass paintings of those years record what he saw. At the Bauhaus in Weimar he was allocated a studio on the second floor of the school building. The family occupied a flat in the 'arm Horn' road; every morning Klee and his son, who now worked in the carpentry workshop, walked to school through the Goethepark, watching the ducks on the river Ilm and the birds in the trees, and looking at plants and nearby buildings. In July 1926 the family moved into the Gropius-designed 'master-house' in Dessau, one semi-detached half of three pairs built by the city for the Bauhaus staff. The Kandinskys occupied the other half. Klee now had a large, properly designed studio almost square in plan, with a large window and one wall entirely painted matt black. He successfully resisted having a telephone installed anywhere near him. When Lily insisted that a telephone was necessary he suggested it should go in the cellar; ultimately they compromised and it was installed by the serving hatch. When Klee resigned from the Bauhaus to fill the post of visiting professor in Düsseldorf he was allowed to retain the master-house, and he used to travel to Düsseldorf for short periods of teaching and live there like a bachelor, cooking for himself and working in an even larger studio. In May 1933 the whole family moved to Düsseldorf but before the end of the year they finally left Germany for Berne. There, one room in a three-room flat was turned into a studio: 'My father was well able to work in his improvised atelier. Nothing disturbed his peace and he was able to concentrate wholly on his work' (FK 109).

Several people have recorded their impressions of Klee in his studio, sometimes at considerable length. Here are some excerpts:

There was a strong smell, an attractive combination of coffee, tobacco, size, oil paints, fine French varnishes, lacquer, methylated spirits, mysterious mixtures. A blue cloud arose from the short pipe before Paul Klee's face. Through the smoke his large dark eyes looked at me quietly... Leaning against the wall there were many small pictures, their faces to the wall. In the middle of the studio stood three easels side by side, on each of them a small picture, unfinished. Paul Klee liked to work at several paintings at one time and walked from one to another, putting touches of colour on this or on that. To one side, near the basin, you could see various tables and, on them, paint boxes, palettes, tubes, pots of colour, size solutions in shallow dishes, chalk solutions and strange pastes, a methylated spirits burner, long and short brushes with thick or thin bristles or hair, spatulas of all kinds... (Lothar Schreyer, *Erinnerungen an Sturm und Bauhaus*, Munich 1956. Schreyer worked at the Bauhaus from 1921 to 1923. In his contribution to EPK he speaks of 'five paintings side by side', EPK 109).

One of the most instructive descriptions of Klee at work is that of Jankel Adler:

In 1931 I was often with Klee. We both had studios in the Düsseldorf Academy... He spent days on preparing a small canvas and then glued it down on pieces of plywood or cardboard in the same way as the old Sienese masters did it. Thus a painting began for him with the preparation of the canvas and was complete only when the frame was finished. So it was not merely an 'art object' but a completed totality. Before he began to draw he would stare for a long time at the prepared canvas... He listened, and it spoke to him through his eyes. And in this way the canvas achieved life through him many years after it was woven.

Never have I seen anyone who had such a creative calm as Klee: it shone from him like the sun. He was a man who knew of day and night, of sky, sea and air. But he did not speak of them; this he could not do. Our language does not suffice to express such things, and so he had to find sign, colour or form.

His studio was spacious but of Spartan simplicity. It would not be true to say, though, that it was therefore empty. Sometimes when I entered I was met by a savoury smell of soup rising from the methylated spirits cooker on which he was preparing his meal. One side of the room was completely occupied by the window. From this window you could look across the garden of the academy. A tangle of gnarled, spreading twigs and crippled grey branches impeded the view. Between them there were little gaps through which you could see the ramp of the bridge over the Rhine to Oberkassel. On the other side you could see a little hill, popularly known as the 'Napoleonsberg'. Strange trees grew on it up into the light and covered the horizon. Standing in the street I have often seen Klee with the pale oval of his face, resembling an enormous egg, pressed against the panes. From below he looked like a ghost. Perhaps he was trying to decipher the language of the twigs in front of his window (EPK 103–4).

KLEE THE TEACHER

Already in 1902 Klee wrote down 'various art-didactic matters' (J 416). In 1908 he taught life drawing at the Debschitz art school in Munich. From 1921 until 1931 he taught at the Bauhaus, and then he worked as visiting professor at the art academy in Düsseldorf until he left Germany in 1933.

He was not the sort of person to find teaching easy. Just as he said little about his own work to visitors and friends, so in teaching he did not speak easily unless he was thoroughly prepared. To this fact, arising partly from innate diffidence and partly from the high standard he demanded from himself, we owe the existence of his lecture notes which have recently been published together with other writings as *The Thinking Eye* (edited by Jürg Spiller, London 1961; German edition *Das bildnerische Denken*, Basle and Stuttgart 1956).

We also have one or two descriptions of Klee lecturing and Klee teaching in the studio, written by his students, from which the following excerpts are taken:

During the first hour we were told to draw a leaf. Some of the students smiled indulgently at this all too easy task. Walking up and down slowly Klee spoke a few words, softly, with long silences. After that we all felt without exception that we had never seen a leaf, or rather the leaf, the essential leaf. He made us feel how the life flows through its large and small veins, how in this way the leaf's form is determined, and how the cellular membrane lightly links these veins like a net... Whether it was an apple, a snail's shell or man (in life drawing), it was always the same: the need to enter into the secret of the creative drive to form, to trace back deliberately and intensively the path of creation from the mature organism to its origin, in so far as insight into these secrets is given to man. (Marianne Ahlfeld-Heymann, student at the Bauhaus, Weimar, 1924; EPK 64–5).

As I thought back over the years it became clear to me that Klee in a short time put students on the road to new experiences — through the exercises which he proposed sometimes hesitantly, sometimes with clear decisiveness. At the beginning of his lessons he would read for a time from a manuscript, often turning his back to the class and occasionally going to the blackboard to draw a diagram which elucidated what he had read. In doing this he sometimes drew with the left hand and sometimes with the right, entirely as the field of blackboard seemed to demand it, sometimes even with both hands at the same time. There was something laconic, even monotonous about his delivery, but in the shift of monotony the richness of his ideas stood out all the more clearly. He was utterly averse to making a theatre of the classroom. (Alexander 'Xanti' Schawinsky, student at the Bauhaus till 1926 and subsequently post-graduate student and assistant teacher in the theatre-workshop; EPK 69).

Klee's pedagogical work at the Bauhaus divided itself into the demonstration of his form theory (in the second and third semesters) and pictorial analysis (in the painting class). Klee's theory of form... is as complex and endless as life itself. It is the product of a rich creative life. Like a conjurer, using glance, word and gesture — all three means of expression being allowed to work with equal intensity — he converted for us the unreal into the real, the irrational into the rational. Things which could have existence only through sensations suddenly became graphically definable... At first it was not always easy to follow him with comprehension. But gradually we came to understand that here somebody was speaking to us of real life. We could experience with him the development of human existence in all its fantasy. We accompanied him through millenia. Archetypal experiences, until then barred to us by mechanical training, Klee opened up to us. (Christof Hertel, student at the Bauhaus; died before completing his studies; wrote this appreciation of Klee as teacher for a special issue of the *Bauhauszeitschrift*, December 1931; EPK 97–8).

Klee is reported to have said to his students that, rather than draw a salary from the school, he ought to be paying them in recompense for all they had taught him. It is perhaps fair to say that, although remarks of this kind are scarcely unprecedented, when meant they reveal the vital teacher.

KLEE AND MUSIC

Reference is frequently made to Klee's affection for music and to his skill as a violinist. It may be well to summarise here what his relationship to this art was, both because music clearly was an important element in Klee's personality and because he worked at a time when artists were fond of finding analogies between their painting and music with, usually, only a very limited understanding of the latter.

Klee's father was a musician and teacher of music. Paul Klee played the violin and occasionally (from 1905 on) the viola. His wife played and taught piano. As a young man Klee played frequently in the Berne orchestra; with friends he frequently played chamber music (first or second violin or viola) at home and sometimes in public. In 1914 he had occasion to play with the professionals Barjansky (cello) and Sapellnikof (piano). His comments on the occasion reveal his impatience with the more-feeling-than-accuracy enthusiasm of most amateurs: 'Idealists drunk with beauty at the expense of intonation, and elegant tricksters at the expense of sincerity' (J 924). Typical also is Klee's comment when, after the artist Kubin had visited him in Munich and they had listened to music together, Klee asked himself: is he really musical? 'I am suspicious of his comment that music excites him too much' (J 888; 1911).

Klee's special passion for the music of Mozart is well known. It was paralleled by deep understanding and knowledge. Romantic music, after the late chamber works of Beethoven, seemed to him uncontrolled and wasteful. He also had a great love for Bach, which appears to have deepened during the war years: 'Never have I experienced Bach with such intensity, never have I felt myself so much at one with him. What concentration, what solitary ultimate enrichment!' (J 1124; 1918). Lyonel Feininger, himself a fine musician, recalls with especial warmth an evening on which Klee played the violin part of Bach's fourth suite: 'No one grasped and brought out the spirit of this piece as firmly as he, without the slightest stressing of the emotional; pure musical structure (EPK 75).

Klee was also interested in the work of modern composers. Feininger speaks of performances of music by César Franck, Ravel, Debussy, Stravinsky and Hindemith. Mahler and Bruckner, the great modern romantics, displeased Klee, while Schönberg interested and excited him.

Like others Klee considered music in some respects analogous to painting. Unlike others (and this illuminates his conception of painting) he considered both arts temporal.

KLEE THE POET

Apart from having general poetic inclinations which could find expression in form and colour Klee had considerable literary gifts, reinforced by his love of reading and the theatre. In 1898 he wrote a group of stories; in 1900 he tried his hand on some dramatic scenes; in 1903–4 he wrote newspaper reviews of plays, operas and concerts; in 1911–12 he wrote exhibition reviews for the Swiss paper *Die Alpen*. In addition to this there are his professional writings as artist and teacher, particularly the *Creative Credo* of 1920, the *Pedagogical Sketchbook* of 1925, and the lecture he gave in Jena in 1924 in connection with an exhibition of his work (an English translation was published in 1947 as *Klee on Modern Art*). Klee wrote in his journal: 'Being a poet and writing poetry are two different things' (J 172; 1901), but it is no surprise to us, seeing Klee principally as an artist, that he wrote poetry as well. Alone, the titles he gave many of his works announce a poet's talent. In fact Klee wrote (or kept) a fair amount of poetry, some of it in his journal and some in a small blue exercise-book that was discovered only after his death. Felix Klee has recently published the collected poems in Switzerland (*Paul Klee: Gedichte*, Verlag Die Arche, Zürich 1960), in some cases printing as verse poetic passages that his father set down as prose. Here are translations of selected items from this collection; those that were originally prose have been set as prose.

A kind of Prometheus. I come before you, Zeus, because I have the strength. You have favoured me; that impels me towards you. Wise enough to surmise you behind all things, I seek not the mighty but the good god. Now I hear your voice out of the cloud: You torture yourself, Prometheus. Tortures have always been my lot since

I was born to love. Often — questioning, entreating — have I lifted my eyes to you: in vain!

So let the strength of my derision beat on your door. If I am not enough for you I leave you this boast. Great are you, great is your work, but great only in the inception, not concluded. A fragment. Conclude! Then I will hail you. Salute the space, the law that measures it. But I do not cry hail. Only the man who struggles receives my Yes. And the greatest among them am I who struggle with divinity. For all my pains and the pains of many I condemn you that you did not conclude. Your best child condemns you, your boldest spirit, your kin yet turned away. (J 180; 1901).

Satirical opus:

The happy man is half an idiot for whom all things flourish and bear fruit. He stands on his little estate, one hand holding a watering-can, the other pointing to himself as the navel of the world. Things sprout and blossom. Boughs heavy with fruit bend towards him. (J 316; 1901). It is clear that these lines are a description of a picture done, as he indicates, on cardboard with grey chalk base, tempera and watercolour).

Sensuality is the pliancy of the flesh under a higher compulsion. Eyes blinded by colour. Ears bathing in sound. Nose in scents. So is it also with the organs of love. (J 364; 1902).

Looking at a tree:
The birds are to be envied
they avoid
all thought of trunk and roots,
and self-content they nimbly swing all day
singing on far outbranching twigs. (J 466; 1902).

For the family tree d'un homme triste: This man has ever shunned the eating of fleshly flesh. He has only sniffed at it; meanwhile he remains pure and much too timorous for action. (J 466; 1902).

The large animals sit mournfully at table and are not satisfied. But the crafty little flies climb about on mountains of bread and inhabit cities of butter. (J 935; 1914).

Dream: I find my house empty, the wine drunk, the stream filled, my naked one taken away, the epitaph wiped off. White on white. (J 946; 1914).

August.
Because I came, blossoms unlocked themselves,
Fullness surrounds me because I am.
The song of the nightingale conjures my ear
To its very heart.
I am father to all,
To all on the stars,
And in the furthest reaches.

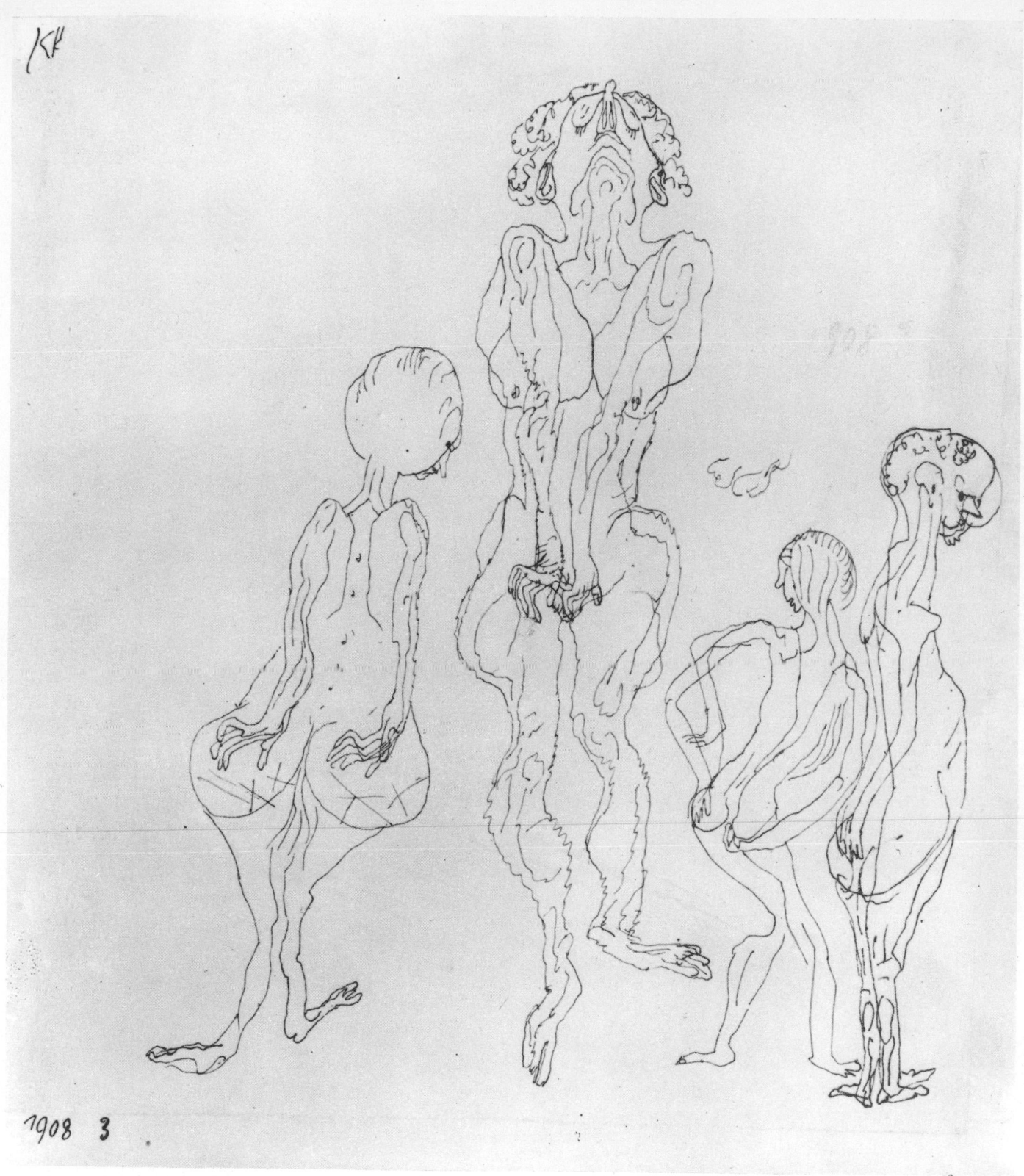

Four nudes: mother and children afraid of father's return

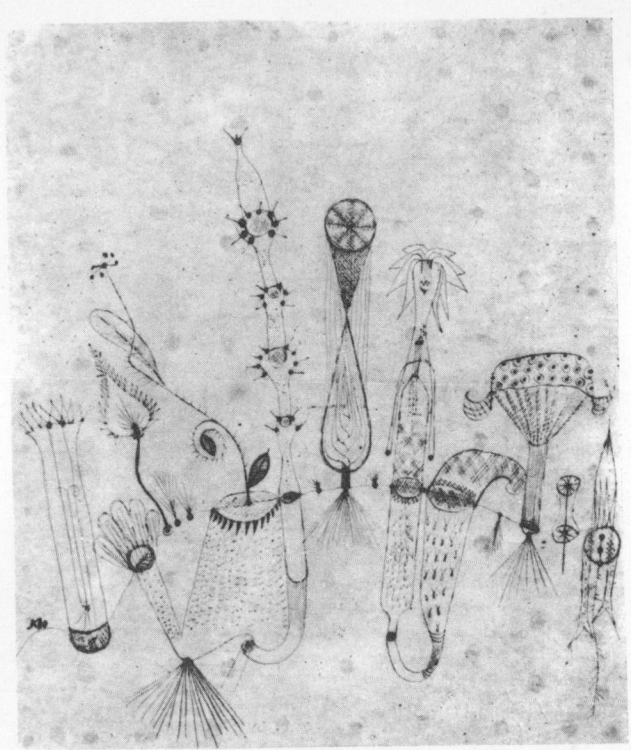

Sketch for 'The realm of plants, earth and air'

Waking from a dream

And
Because I went, evening fell
And a mantle of clouds
Sheathed in the light.
Because I went,
Nothing casts its shadow
Over all.
O thorn
In the silver swelling fruit! (J 1081a; 1917).

Once emerged from the grey of night
Then heavy and precious
and strong from the fire
in the evening filled with God and bowed
Ethereally now rained round with blue
Floating off over mountains' snow caps
to wise constellations.

(This is the text of the picture-poem 1918 No. 17,
presumably written by Klee himself. See plate 10.)

Notes on the illustrations

In 1919 Klee drew at least three self-portraits, including this one. Its frontality, frequent in his drawings and paintings of heads, allows for great formal simplicity within which the wiry lines of beard, hair and eyebrows, and the thin, nervous lines forming mouth and nose (the latter looking much like one of Klee's studies of roots), can play particularly powerful roles. 'My human faces', wrote Klee 'are truer than the real ones'.

Abstract linear constructions, visual signs, and hints of representation together present an entirely original kind of art.

One of the sharpest of Klee's satirical works, related in subject to Invention 7, *A man grovelling before the crown*. A very finely worked plate, the second attempt at etching this particular subject.

Klee's name does not appear in surveys of modern sculpture, and indeed he produced very little. In 1906, a little to his own surprise, he bought a modelling table and some plaster; in 1918 his journal (1102) records his recognition of the sculptural value of stones and waterworn tiles. The sculptures illustrated here were done between 1915 and 1920. In the early twenties he made at least thirty *Kasperlfiguren* (hand puppets) for his son Felix: an amazing troupe of characters, including a German Nationalist, a Buddhist monk, the Barber of Bagdad, a white-haired Eskimo, and the match-box ghost, made out of roughly carved bits of wood, plaster, electric plugs, etc. (they are illustrated in FK). He returned to sculpture briefly in 1932. The general impression is one of lighthearted, uninhibited invention of three-dimensional images, free of technical and formal conventions, anticipating several aspects of Picasso's sculpture of the 1930's.

Klee's journal, January 1905 (585): '*Hero with a wing*, a tragicomic hero, perhaps an antique Don Quixote. This formula and poetic idea, which came up boggily in November 1904, is now finally drained off and consolidated. In contrast to divine beings, this man has been born with only one angel's wing, and makes incessant attempts to fly. In the process he breaks arm and leg, but nevertheless perseveres under the banner of his idea. The antithesis between his monumental, solemn pose and his already ruinous condition, needed particularly to be set down as symbol of the tragicomic.'

Although he produced much of great value earlier, it seems to me that Klee achieved complete maturity as a draughtsman in this year, 1911, with drawings of this kind. *Jugendstil* and expressionist elements have been completely assimilated, and he has evolved for himself a graphic language that can serve representational ends without at all conflicting with his abstract functions or with his expressive needs. He draws chiefly with short, thin, brittle lines which gradually capture the object's appearance rather than delineate it—a manner derived probably from his own experience as etcher. This drawing is one of a series of Munich's *Hauptbahnhof* done in 1911; other drawings of this year include the twenty-six drawings for *Candide* in which the same graphic manner is applied to more fantastic and satirical ends.

Drawings of this kind probably began as an aimless play of lines, a kind of knitting with the pen, that soon acquired architectural character and so was encouraged to grow into a monumental group of buildings.

One of the most powerful of all Klee's drawings, and one that, in its simple vehemence and in the strength of its calligraphic marks, looks utterly new today.

Page 25 *Portrait of an expressionist*, 1922/240. Tempera on paper $12\frac{1}{8} \times 8\frac{3}{4}$ in. $(31 \times 22.2$ cm.$)$. New York, Mrs Jane Wade Lombard.

This is presumably a self-portrait—in which case the satirical intent indicated in the title and in the drawing itself becomes self-critical. Although a man of passionate feelings, Klee was not an Expressionist: except in a few early graphic works he sought always to transmute specific and possibly discordant emotions into more universal, ultimately harmonious, statements, and it is my impression that he was unsympathetic to the more naked phenomena of Expressionism in others. He may here, then, be ridiculing a repressed tendency in himself; he may also be making a comment on the artistic milieu in which he existed at this time, the Bauhaus, where in 1922 Romantic and Expressionist attitudes still dominated.

Page 35 *Four nudes: mother and children afraid of father's return*. 1908/3. Pen. $6\frac{5}{8} \times 5\frac{7}{8}$ in. $(17 \times 15$ cm.$)$. London, Lady Hulton.

One of Klee's most Expressionist works. The fine lines, and the distorted human images they make, convey a partly humorous, partly tragic effect. The drawing is subtitled 'Design for Bloesch's epic poem'. Hans Bloesch had been Klee's friend since his Berne school days. He was a writer and librarian, accompanied Klee to Paris in 1905, visited him in Munich, and befriended him later again in Berne. It does not appear that the collaboration indicated here ever grew into a publishable work.

Page 36 *Sketch for 'The realm of plants, earth and air'*, 1920/205. Pen. $8\frac{3}{8} \times 7\frac{1}{2}$ in. $(22.5 \times 19$ cm.$)$. Berne, Klee Foundation.

From his study of plants—one is tempted to say, his empathy into the life of plants—Klee learnt to make linear plants flourish on paper, with something of the inevitability of nature's own. A painting based on this drawing followed in 1921.

Page 36 *Waking from a dream*, 1932/z.4. Brush drawing. $12\frac{1}{2} \times 16\frac{3}{4}$ in. $(32.2 \times 42.8$ cm.$)$. Berne, Klee Foundation.

An action drawing? Out of the jungle of rapid brush-strokes emerges a suggestion of a figure, reclining.

COLOUR PLATES

Plate 1 *Group of trees*, 1899. Oil. $13\frac{3}{4} \times 19\frac{1}{4}$ in. $(34.9 \times 48.7$ cm.$)$. Berne, Klee Foundation.

In 1899 Klee bought his first box of oil paints. He made his first essays in the medium during a month's holiday in Burghausen: 'I found painting difficult, but I soon acquired a certain dexterity in it and threw off some bold studies' (J 70). This painting suggests some sympathy with the German brand of Impressionism which harbours elements of Expressionism.

Plate 2 *Garden scene with watering-can*, 1905/24, *(Gartenszene mit der Giesskanne)*. Watercolour on glass. $5\frac{1}{8} \times 7\frac{1}{8}$ in. $(13.1 \times 18.1$ cm.$)$. Berne, Felix Klee.

One of twenty-six drawings and watercolours on glass done in 1905–6. They tend to be stylistically freer works than his contemporary etchings, calm in mood and naturalistic in form. The *Garden scene* is the freshest of them. In its use of bright red and, generally, its emphasis on the decorative properties of colour and line, it suggests some contact with Fauvism, but of this French movement Klee, at this time, knew nothing.

Plate 3 *Girl with jugs*, 1910/120, *(Mädchen mit Krügen)*. Oil on panel. $13\frac{1}{2} \times 10\frac{5}{8}$ in. $(34.5 \times 27$ cm.$)$. Berne, Felix Klee.

The first clear statement of Klee's debt to Cézanne, done at a time when Klee was making particularly rapid progress towards a full understanding of the function of colour (see the Introduction). The, for him, uncharacteristically brash handling of the thin paint suggests the violence of German Expressionism but may be Fauve in origin; in some passages, most noticeably in the girl's right cheek, the brashness makes way for a deliberate juxtaposing of parallel brush-strokes that comes from Cézanne.

Plate 4 *Sun in the courtyard*, 1913, *(Sonne im Hof)*. Watercolour. $7\frac{3}{4} \times 4\frac{3}{4}$ in. $(19.7 \times 12$ cm.$)$. London, Lady Hulton.

In 1912 Klee had visited Delaunay; in 1913 he saw a collection of works by Emil Nolde. This little watercolour owes something to both artists, and most perhaps to Delaunay's paintings of the *Eiffel Tower* kind, in which not only the colour but also the rhythmically distorted form is used to convey a sense of excitement.

Plate 5 *Little port*, 1914/146, *(Kleiner Hafen)*. Watercolour. $6\frac{1}{8} \times 5\frac{1}{2}$ in. $(15.6 \times 14$ cm.$)$. Berne, Felix Klee.

Done presumably before the visit to Africa. A delicate little picture, suggesting Chinese landscape painting in its use of broad areas focussing on one sharp detail, the jetty, which becomes the compositional hinge and gives a feeling of scale. In terms of colour, it shows Klee at his closest to Fauvism.

Plate 6 *Before the gates of Kairouan*, 1914/216, *(Vor den Toren von Kairouan)*. Watercolour. $8\frac{1}{2} \times 12\frac{1}{2}$ in. $(21.5 \times 31.5$ cm.$)$. Berne, Klee Foundation.

One of the watercolours done by Klee in North Africa, directly from the motif. These works show a dramatic advance over his earlier efforts: the experience of North Africa enabled him to make free and personal use of what he had learnt from Cézanne and Delaunay. In its colour planes and the little squiggles signifying animals, this little work establishes some of the themes that will occupy him for the rest of his life (see, for instance, plate 43, *With the two lost ones*, 1938).

Plate 7 *Homage to Picasso*, 1914/192, *(Hommage à Picasso)*. Oil on panel. $15 \times 11\frac{3}{4}$ in. $(38 \times 30$ cm.$)$. Cos Cob, Connecticut, P.A. Rübel.

Grohmann says that Klee entitled this picture to indicate that 'it seemed to him to be on the same level' as Picasso's works. If this is right, it suggests a challenge rather than homage, and there is no evidence that Klee felt it necessary thus to measure himself against his contemporaries. He had seen work by Picasso in Paris (in Wilhelm Uhde's collection and in Kahnweiler's gallery) and in Munich exhibitions from 1910 on. Nevertheless this painting owes little to Picasso beyond the oval format; stylistically it is much closer to Delaunay although it has a density of colour and texture uncharacteristic of the Frenchman and indicative of much overpainting. Picasso visited Klee in Berne in November 1937; in 1951 he described Klee, cryptically, as 'Pascal-Napoleon'.

Plate 8 *Motif from Hamamet*, 1914/48, *(Motif aus Hamamet)*. Watercolour. $7\frac{7}{8} \times 6$ in. $(20 \times 15.5$ cm.$)$. Basle, R. Kupferstichkabinett, R. Doetsch-Benziger Bequest.

It is not clear whether this watercolour was produced in Africa or whether it is one of those in which Klee, back in Munich, based himself on memories and watercolours of Africa. Here the subject—the light, formal character and spirit of Hamamet has been translated into almost completely abstract terms, the rhythmic disposition of colour areas and the light that comes from them, and the texture of the paper, and of some of the brush strokes, creating an equivalent sensation to the original.

Plate 9 *Wings for 'Anatomy of Aphrodite'*, 1915/48, *(Flügelstücke zur Anatomie der Aphrodite)*. Watercolour. $9\frac{1}{4} \times 3\frac{3}{8}$ and $9\frac{1}{4} \times 4\frac{3}{4}$ in. $(23.6 \times 8.4$ and 23.4×12.1 cm.$)$. Berne, Felix Klee.

These two watercolours have hitherto been published as *Anatomy of Aphrodite* but are in fact to be imagined as the wings of a triptych whose centrepiece Klee catalogued as '1915/45'. They come amongst Klee's first completely abstract works, and show him at his closest to the last works of his friend Franz Marc.

Plate 10 *Once emerged from the grey of night*, 1918/17, *(Einst dem Grau der Nacht enttaucht...)*. Watercolour and collage. $9\frac{7}{8} \times 6$ in. $(25.1 \times 15.5$ cm.$)$. Berne, Klee Foundation.

A unique combination of picture and poem. The colours modulate to fit the sense of the words very much in the way the pattern of a Schubert accompaniment may modulate to suit the changing mood of a song. The horizontal band of silver-printed paper marks a break in the poem and corresponds to the double bar (//) in Klee's written version at the top of the mount. This fusion of poetry, pattern, letter forms and colour is entirely original but echoes the synaesthetic interests of Symbolist poetry and painting. A translation of the poem is given on page 37.

Plate 11 *Garden at night*, 1918/55, *(Garten nachts)*. Gouache. $9\frac{7}{8} \times 4\frac{7}{8}$ in. $(25.1 \times 12.3$ cm.$)$. London, Lady Hulton.

The *Märchen* or traditional fairy-tale played an important role in the development of German Romantic literature. To Klee it offered an alternative to the primitivist interests of some German Expressionists (notably Schmidt-Rottluff and

Pechstein) and overlapped with the child art he valued so highly. The word *märchenhaft* appears frequently in Klee's writings as a quality he sought to achieve, and in his work dreamily poetic pictures like this one appear side by side with more architectonic and classical ones. Their coexistence is an essential attribute of Klee's artistic life.

Plate 12 *Hermitage*, 1918/61, *(Einsidelei)*. Watercolour on chalk ground. $7\frac{1}{4} \times 10$ in. $(18.5 \times 25.5$ cm.$)$. Berne, Klee Foundation.

Another instance of Klee in pursuit of the *märchenhaft*. Here the draped curtains indicated at the top of the picture have the effect of lifting Klee's dream images on to the semi-real level of the stage.

Plate 13 *Women's pavilion*, 1921/191, *(Der Frauen Pavillon)*. Oil on panel. $15\frac{3}{4} \times 20\frac{1}{8}$ in. $(40 \times 51$ cm.$)$. New York, Ralph Colin.

Polyphony of circular and angular forms set on stave-like lines, in muted colours that range from near black to an almost white pale blue. This is one of several such pictures, using more or less horizontal lines and tree and hill shapes, done by Klee around this year.

Plate 14 *Vocal fabric of the singer Rosa Silber*, 1922/126. Gouache and gesso on canvas. $20\frac{1}{2} \times 16\frac{1}{2}$ in. $(52 \times 42$ cm.$)$. New York, Museum of Modern Art.

The initials R.S., letters to represent the five vowels, small areas of off-hand patterning, float over a field of colours that pivot on white. A picture curiously difficult to connect with any other phenomenon in the art of Klee's time. Cubism had used letters, of course, but for rather different purposes. Some of Kurt Schwitters' most delicate collages (later in date than this Klee) have something of the same finesse and allusiveness.

Plate 15 *Senecio*, 1922/181. Oil on linen. 16×15 in $(39.8 \times 38$ cm.$)$. Basle, Kunstmuseum.

The head seen frontally is a recurring theme in Klee's paintings and drawings. Here, in one of Klee's finest paintings, it is seen in terms of the interaction of simple geometrical forms (set down with characteristic imprecision) and idiosyncratic colour. Note the importance of texture and of the sharp lines that mark the eyes. One is tempted to relate this picture to the Bauhaus's insistence on simple geometrical shapes, but in fact *Senecio* predates the emergence of this Bauhaus attitude, and anyway the particular quality of this picture resides in its balance of clear against nebulous form and its reliance on subtle colours far removed from the primaries predominantly used at the Bauhaus after 1923.

Plate 16 *The god of the northern forest*, 1922/32, *(Der Gott des nördlichen Waldes)*. Oil on canvas on cardboard. $20\frac{7}{8} \times 16\frac{1}{2}$ in. $(53 \times 41.2$ cm.$)$. Berne, Klee Foundation.

The head of the god emerges out of its loosely patterned setting in terms of analytical Cubism at its most hermetic: a few planes, projecting on account of the light blue that acts as highlights rather than because of their construction, are sufficient to suggest the head and to emphasise its existence *in* and as part of the forest.

Plate 17 *Ambassador of autumn*, 1922/69, *(Der Bote des Herbsts)*. Watercolour. $10\frac{3}{8} \times 12\frac{3}{4}$ in. (26.4 × 31.7 cm.). New Haven, Connecticut, Yale University Art Gallery.

One of the finest works of a remarkably fruitful year. Out of delicately set down scales of blue watercolour, reminiscent of the Bauhaus students' exercises in tone but moving around the colour circle towards green and red, and by adding the tree symbol in complementary orange, Klee has created a remarkably unmechanical, delicate image and then enriched it by means of a title full of associative images.

Plate 18 *Seventeen, crazy*, 1923/156, *(Siebzehn, irr)*. Pen and watercolour. $8\frac{7}{8} \times 11\frac{1}{4}$ in. (22.5 × 28.5 cm.). Basle, Kunstmuseum, R. Doetsch-Benziger Bequest.

An extremely original mixture of anthropomorphic suggestions, abstract visual signs and letters, with the title incorporated in the picture itself, the whole intended to convey, I imagine, the character of adolescent disquiet.

Plate 19 *Battle scene from the comic fantastic opera 'The Seafarer'*, 1923/123, *(Kampfszene aus der komisch-phantastischen Oper 'Der Seefahrer')*. Watercolour and oil on paper. $15 \times 20\frac{3}{8}$ in. (38 × 51.5 cm.). Muttenz bei Basel, Mrs. T. Durst-Haass.

An exercise in tonal gradations as basis for the confrontation of freely invented images representing man, boat and monsters.

Plate 20 *Mural painting*, 1924/128, *(Wandbild)*. Tempera on canvas. $10 \times 21\frac{3}{4}$ in. (25 × 54 cm.). Berne, Klee Foundation.

The title is not to be taken literally: this is a small picture. Klee may have thought it capable of being the basis for a wall-sized work (at the Bauhaus Kandinsky and Schlemmer were investigating the possibilities of modern mural painting); he may also have meant to point to the architectural allusions included in the white-line pattern. One tends not to notice the subtlety and complexity of the colour: the colourist and the graphic magician collaborate here.

Plate 21 *Mountains in winter*, 1925/3, *(Gebirge im Winter)*. Sprayed watercolour and brush. $11 \times 14\frac{1}{2}$ in. (28 × 36.5 cm.). Berne, Hermann Rupf.

Klee first used the spray technique (here combined with masking) in 1924. It is probable that various artists at the Bauhaus recognised the atomizer as a potential painting instrument about that time but, in so far as it is possible to check this at present, Klee appears to have been the first. The crystalline mountain forms offer a dramatic setting for the delicate, seaweed-like tree. The inscription at bottom left—date, number and title—is balanced by abstract inscription-like marks on the right.

Plate 22 *Fish magic*, 1925/R.5, *(Fischzauber)*. Oil and watercolour, varnished. $30\frac{1}{4} \times 38\frac{5}{8}$ in. (76.3 × 98.2 cm.). Philadelphia, Museum of Art, The Louise and Walter Arensberg Collection.

A pictorial fairytale of the utmost delicacy in line, colour and texture. One recalls the aquarium Klee had visited with so much pleasure in Naples but this is not merely a picture of fishes in a tank, nor even a poetic version of such a representation, but a totally fantastic creation of great richness. Flowers, figures, the sun, the moon and a cock cohabit this world in colourful harmony. An unusually large picture for Klee at this time.

Plate 23 *Ancient sound*, 1925/X.6, *(Alter Klang)*. Oil on cardboard. 15×15 in. (38 × 38 cm.). Basle, Kunstmuseum, R. Doetsch-Benziger Bequest.

Klee began to paint his so-called 'Magic Squares' in 1922, but they should be seen as descendants from the North African watercolours with their rectangular colour planes, and from such paintings as *Invention (with the dovecote)* (1917) and *Once emerged from the grey of night* (1918, plate 10). Obviously colour is the most effective element in pictures of this kind, but much depends also on the size of the squares, any variation in their size, and any departure from the basic vertical-horizontal construction. Some of Klee's 'magic squares' pictures are done very precisely, possibly with a dark line separating each colour square from the next; others are done freely and often break the pattern blatantly or, as in this case, surreptitiously.

Plate 24 *The golden fish*, 1925/R.5, *(Der goldene Fisch)*. Oil and watercolour on cardboard. $19\frac{1}{8} \times 27$ in. (48.5 × 68.5 cm.). Hamburg, Kunsthalle.

Another fish picture, one in which the yellow and red of the central fish shines out in contrast to the dark ground on which it is painted. Smaller fish hover near the edges, together with typical Klee signs for plants.

Plate 25 *Harmony of the northern flora*, 1927/E.4, *(Harmonie der nördlichen Flora)*. Oil on cardboard. (Dimensions unobtainable). Berne, Felix Klee.

Here, in contrast to *Ancient sound* (plate 23) Klee's colour areas are carefully organised. Because of this, one is tempted to relate a picture like this one to the kind of paintings Mondrian was producing in 1919–20—canvases neatly covered with small, equal colour areas like tiles. By 1923–4 Klee must certainly have known Mondrian's work, though whether he would have known any Mondrians of this particular kind is questionable. The chief difference between them is that Mondrian sought to create so complete a balance of colours that the ultimate picture tends almost to be grey as a result of its utter egalitarianism, whereas Klee liked to give his pictures dominant passages and colours. In this particular picture he has surrounded a centre area of predominantly warm colours with a margin of predominantly cool colours, and the centre is also more luminous than the margin. Such a picture can be read almost as, say, a minuet and trio, one phase succeeding another, with a change in key as well as in rhythm.

Plate 26 *A leaf from the town records*, 1928/N.6, *(Ein*

Blatt aus dem Städtebuch). Oil on gesso, on paper on wood. 17 × 12⅜ in. (42.5 × 31.5 cm.). Basle, Kunstmuseum.

The pattern of lines resembles that of *Mural painting* (plate 20) and variations of it appear in several of Klee's paintings and drawings. Here, presented as on a sealed tablet, the pattern takes on the character of hieroglyphics. Note the importance of the yellow wood background.

Plate 27 *Italian town*, 1928/P.6, *(Italienische Stadt)*. Watercolour on paper on cardboard. 13⅜ × 9¼ in. (34.3 × 23.6 cm.). Berne, Felix Klee.

Klee lectured on perspective at the Bauhaus in 1921 and about the same time began to produce pictures in which a consistent perspective construction (or, as in some of them, conflicting perspectives) play a dominant role. Such pictures continue to occur in his work throughout the 1920s. Clearly it was not his intention to reject the colour space of Cézanne. In so far as he used perspective to create any illusion of space, he almost completely negated this illusion by other means—in this picture through his disposition of colours which, on account of their tonal values, work in opposition to the directions indicated by the linear construction. It is probably this linear-construction aspect of perspective that attracted Klee to it, and this will have been supported by his feeling for architecture and townscape. In Klee's hands perspective becomes a constructive means of 'taking a line for a walk'.

Plate 28 *Monument in fertile country*, 1929/N.1, *(Monument in Fruchtland)*. Watercolour. 18½ × 12 in. (46 × 30.5 cm). Berne, Klee Foundation.

Klee was in Egypt from December 17, 1928, to January 17, 1929. He wrote to Lily, his wife, on April 17, 1929, concerning this picture: 'I am painting a landscape somewhat like the view of the fertile country from the distant mountains of the Valley of the Kings. The polyphonic interplay between earth and atmosphere has been kept as fluid as possible'. His abstract arrangement of coloured stripes manages to suggest temperature, terrain, space and movement.

Plate 29 *Table of colour (in grey major)*, 1930/R3, *(Farbtafel auf maiorem Grau)*. Pastel with glue on paper on cardboard. 15¾ × 11¾ in. (39.8 × 29.6 cm.). Berne, Klee Foundation.

The musical analogy is apt: Klee places colour-squares into his picture space like sounds. Like the notes of Webern, each has its own value and sounds clearly, although it is conditioned by adjacent sounds or colours. One tends to think of Klee's chequer-board patterns as formally negative, as merely vehicles for colour juxtaposition, but of course the very tidiness of the organisation has its own expressive power and, what is more, the colour areas are not all equal in size. Each storey is a little higher than the preceding one. The result of this is a lightening and lifting of the whole construction. The specific location of the colours within the pattern is of great importance. A surprising range of different effects results from seeing the picture turned upside down or sideways.

Plate 30 *Individualized measurement of strata*, 1930/R.2, *(Individualisierte Höhenmessung der Lagen)*. Pastel on paste ground. 19 × 14 in. (48.3 × 35.5 cm.). Berne, Klee Foundation.

One of the most sonorous of Klee's colour compositions, and probably to be seen as one of his pictures recalling impressions of Egypt. It seems to me unnecessarily interpretative to say, as Grohmann does, that 'The green stripe at the bottom of the picture is the Nile and the light ochre stripe on top is a hill'. It is not likely that Klee's intention was to be as specific as that. What matters is the subtlety and the rareness of these particular colour confrontations and the effectiveness of the rhythmic grouping of different shapes and sizes of colour areas.

Plate 31 *Small town among the rocks*, 1932/X.16, *(Kleine Felsenstadt)*. Oil on panel. 17⅜ × 22 in. (44 × 56 cm.). Berne, Klee Foundation.

One of the first paintings to give hints of the more monumental, line plus flat colour style of Klee's last years. An unusual range of colours. Note the plasticity of the top third of the picture as against the more or less flat jig-saw of colours below.

Plate 32 *Polyphony*, 1932/X.13, *(Polyphonie)*. Unvarnished tempera on linen. 26¼ × 41¾ in. (66.5 × 106 cm.). Basle, Kunstmuseum, Emanuel Hoffmann Foundation.

Klee did a series of pictures in 1930–3 which he called Divisionist, in reference to the dots of divided colour used by Seurat and his followers. This is one of them. Klee did not intend to create an optical mixture of colours so much as to add complexity to the colour and space sensation his picture could produce. First he paints a picture not unlike his 'Magic Squares' and then he neatly imposes on the squares rows of dots that seem to hover a little in front of the squares. Not all the dots are different in colour from their backgrounds, and the total effect is one of shimmering insubstantiality.

Plate 33 *Bust of a child*, 1933/380, *(Büste eines Kindes)*. Varnished watercolour on cloth on wood. 20⅛ × 20⅛ in. (51 × 51 cm.). Berne, Klee Foundation.

One of a related group of heads painted about this time, all simple in outline and using more or less arbitrarily placed lines to delimit flat colour areas.

Plate 34 *Reposing Sphinx*, 1934/210, *(Ruhende Sphinx)*. Oil on canvas. 35⅞ × 47⅝ in. (91 × 121 cm.). Berne, Klee Foundation.

Freely meandering lines divide up the picture area into irregular shapes which are then flatly coloured. The sphinx image, one imagines, was discovered and held in the process. The dominant red in the centre is surrounded by a variety of delicately nuanced colours.

Plate 35 *Child consecrated to suffering*, 1935/K.11,

(*W-geweihtes Kind*). Gouache and oil. $5\frac{7}{8} \times 9$ in. $(15 \times 23$ cm.). Buffalo, Albright-Knox Art Gallery.

Rich in colour and texture, though both within a small range. During the following years the black line Klee used here to suggest form and to make pattern grows in weight and gestural significance. Here the intention is principally playful. The line indicating the nose, and those representing the eyebrows are themselves humorous, and the 'W' on the child's brow makes a visual-verbal pun. In German the letter W and word *Weh* (=suffering, sorrow) are pronounced the same; thus 'suffering' is inscribed on the child's forehead.

Plate 36 *Conspicuous might*, 1935/L15, *(Protzige Wehr)*. Watercolour over chalk and limed paper with egg on card. $18\frac{7}{8} \times 12$ in. $(47.5$ cm. $\times 30.5$ cm.). Berne, Klee Foundation.

Klee's love of patterning, with its roots in primitive art, shows clearly here but in an unusual setting. His clanking Mars-figure carrying something like the Order of the Iron Cross in its hand, must be taken to be a symbol of Germany's military resurgence, as seen from Switzerland.

Plate 37 *Will they sit down?* 1935/qu.15, *(Nehmen sie Platz?)*. Charcoal and red crayon. $8\frac{1}{8} \times 11\frac{1}{4}$ in. $(20.8 \times 29.6$ cm.). Berne, Klee Foundation.

A study in the balance of tensions, particularly interesting as a precursor of Klee's late style.

Plate 38 *Picture page*, 1937/Q. 13, *(Bilderbogen)*. Oil on panel. $23\frac{1}{4} \times 22$ in. $(59 \times 56$ cm.). Washington, Phillips Gallery.

A compilation of pictograms, strongly primitive in character but including many motifs familiar from other paintings and drawings by Klee. Painted in a manner to suggest incised and coloured wood but suggestive also of the recent interest in *graffiti* in contemporary art.

Plate 39 *Overland*, 1937/T.5, *(Überland)*. Colour in paste medium and pastel on cloth. (Dimensions unobtainable). Berne, Felix Klee.

One of the most sonorous and harmonious examples of Klee's late style. During 1937—1940 he produced several paintings using strong, discontinuous black lines in combination with flat areas of colour. In some the black lines suggest specific images; here Klee sees in them a general landscape (or map?) effect. The density of the paste medium and the richness of pastel give this, and other late works, a surprising luminosity.

Plate 40 *Thoughts of posterity*, 1937/P.14, *(Gedanken an Nachkommenschaft)*. Charcoal and watercolour, on chalk and gum, on paper on cardboard. $11\frac{3}{8} \times 7\frac{1}{2}$ in. $(29.2 \times 19$ cm.). Berne, Felix Klee.

A light-hearted figurative invention, vaguely reminiscent of Picasso's frequent linear studies of reclining figures, showing a pregnant woman lying on a bed, contemplating an oval portrait, all done with charcoal lines and delicate colour.

Plate 41 *Fruit on a blue ground*, 1938/J.10, *(Früchte auf Blau)*. Colour in paste medium on panel. $21\frac{5}{8} \times 53\frac{1}{2}$ in. $(55 \times 136$ cm.). Berne, Klee Foundation.

One of Klee's largest pictures, all of which belong to his last years. See also the notes on *Overland* (plate 39) and on *Coelin Fruit* (plate 42).

Plate 42 *Coelin fruit*, 1938/D.8, *(Coelin-Frucht)*. Colour in paste medium. $14\frac{1}{8} \times 10\frac{5}{8}$ in. $(35.5 \times 27$ cm.). Berne, Klee Foundation.

A comparison between this picture and *Fruit on a blue ground* (plate 41) shows how, although in both works the black line is used to delineate object-shapes, the character of both line and colour-infilling can vary considerably. In the larger painting the strong and fluid lines make shapes that are evenly filled with colour. Here the line is scratchy, tentative and the colour is roughly put in, not quite filling its areas—this gives a greater degree of vibrancy to both colour and shapes, just as the severity of the composition gives this small work a remarkable monumentality. Klee here uses only five colours (including black) plus the colour of the paper support.

Plate 43 *With the two lost ones*, 1938/D.16, *(Mit den beiden Verirrten)*. Watercolour on newspaper. $12\frac{5}{8} \times 19$ in. $(32 \times 48.5$ cm.). Basle, Kupferstichkabinett, R. Doetsch-Benziger Bequest.

A maze of colour areas and linear obstacles, confronting two little mannikins. One senses that these were introduced last of all, to transform a composition into a subject, or a decoration into a problem. They also of course serve to establish a superhuman scale.

Plate 44 *Flowers in stone*, 1939/GG.18, *(Blumen in Stein)*. Oil on cardboard. $19\frac{5}{8} \times 15\frac{5}{8}$ in. $(50.1 \times 39.6$ cm.). Lucerne, Galerie Rosengart.

Even in Klee's widely ranging output, this is a strange work. It appears to represent a massive stone sculpture of a primitive or primitivist kind, marked with secret signs, each in its little patch of colour. The floor is shown in rough perspective; the sculpture is not shown three-dimensionally although our perceptual habits cause us to imagine it as a thing of mass. The lines and colours at the top of the picture, and its brushwork texture, re-establish its two-dimensionality.

Plate 45 *Accident*, 1939/LM.18, *(Unfall)*. Tempera and crayon and white paint on paper. $26\frac{3}{4} \times 10$ in. $(68 \times 25.5$ cm.) Basle, Ida Meyer-Chagall Collection.

A coloured brush drawing. The *fermata* or pause sign in music acts as compositional counterpart to the woman's head, as overlooking presence, and also, visually and iconographically, as an indication of stillness.

Plate 46 *Naked on the bed*, 1939/A.13, *(Nackt auf dem Bett)*. Watercolour. $8\frac{1}{4} \times 11\frac{5}{8}$ in. $(21.1 \times 29.4$ cm.). Berne, Felix Klee.

The figures are drawn in long, flowing lines that only vaguely indicate the shapes of the bodies and yet unmistakably represent living beings.

Plate 47 *Evening in the suburbs*, 1940/R.7, *(Vorstadt-Abend)*. Oil and tempera on jute. $5\frac{1}{2} \times 13\frac{3}{8}$ in. $(13.9 \times 34.3$ cm.). Berne, Felix Klee.

Just as he investigated varying and mixed media, so also Klee liked to exploit the qualities of different surfaces as support to his painting. The roughness of the jute, and the way the white ground is allowed to show through the painting, are as important as the black lines and the colours between them.

Plate 48 *Still-life on leap day*, 1940/N.13, *(Stilleben am Schalttag)*. Colour in paste medium on panel. $29\frac{1}{8} \times 43\frac{1}{4}$ in. $(74 \times 110$ cm.). Berne, Klee Foundation.

Painted on February 29. A large painting in a minor key of colour—one of those works in which Klee utterly transcends any barriers between abstract and representational art, inventing with astonishing freedom.

Plate 49 *Double*, 1940/N.16, *(Doppel)*. Colour in paste medium. $20\frac{1}{2} \times 13\frac{1}{2}$ in. $(52 \times 34.5$ cm.). Berne, Klee Foundation.

Much the same colours as *Still-life on leap day* (plate 48). One of a number of paintings done in 1939–40 suggestive of stained glass.

Plate 50 *Black, still in place*, 1940/Z.15, *(Schwarz, noch am Ort)*. Unvarnished tempera on canvas. $12 \times 3\frac{3}{4}$ in. $(31 \times 9.5$ cm.). Basle, Kunstmuseum, R. Doetsch-Benziger Bequest.

This small painting is perhaps the most prophetic in Klee's whole output. Painted in the year of his death, at the age of sixty, six or seven years before the emergence of American abstract expressionism. The American movement was born out of the union of abstract painting with Surrealism. Klee had an innate tendency that one could label Surrealism (working from the unconscious, welcoming images of fantasy, exploiting conflicting associations), and the Paris Surrealists had hailed him as a fellow spirit. From Cubism and Kandinsky he inherited abstract painting. So he combined in himself the bases of abstract expressionism. What differentiates the present work from the paintings of the Americans is principally physical size, but it is characteristic of our age that artistic influences should flow at least as much through the scaleless media of the printed reproduction and the lecture-room screen as through contact with the originals.